Intelligence and Intelligibility

G. E. R. Lloyd is Emeritus Professor of Ancient Philosophy and Science at the University of Cambridge. He is the author of twenty-eight books, including *Being, Humanity, and Understanding: Studies in Ancient and Modern Societies* (Oxford 2012) and *The Ideals of Inquiry: An Ancient History* (Oxford 2014). He became a Fellow of the British Academy in 1983 and received the Sarton medal in 1987. Lloyd was elected to an Honorary Fellowship at Kings in 1991, to Honorary Foreign Membership of the American Academy of Arts and Sciences in 1995, to an Honorary Fellowship at Darwin in 2000, and to an Honorary DLitt by Oxford University (2010) and St Andrews University (2016). He was knighted for 'services to the history of thought' in 1997, and received the Kenyon Medal for Classical scholarship from the British Academy in 2007 and the Dan David prize in 2013.

Intelligence and Intelligibility

Cross-Cultural Studies of Human Cognitive Experience

G. E. R. LLOYD

OXFORD
UNIVERSITY PRESS

OXFORD
UNIVERSITY PRESS

Great Clarendon Street, Oxford, OX2 6DP,
United Kingdom

Oxford University Press is a department of the University of Oxford.
It furthers the University's objective of excellence in research, scholarship,
and education by publishing worldwide. Oxford is a registered trade mark of
Oxford University Press in the UK and in certain other countries

First published 2020
First published in paperback 2022

Published in the United States of America by Oxford University Press
198 Madison Avenue, New York, NY 10016, United States of America

British Library Cataloguing in Publication Data
Data available

Library of Congress Cataloging in Publication Data
Data available

ISBN 978-0-19-885459-3 (Hbk.)
ISBN 978-0-19-286731-5 (Pbk.)

Contents

List of Figures

Introduction

In a number of disciplines that include philosophy, history, social anthropology, psychology, cognitive science, and even archaeology, one can detect a certain deep-seated tension. On the one hand, there is an appreciation of the cognitive capacities that all humans have in common, on the other, a recognition of the huge diversity in that regard between different individuals and groups. This tension prompts one to ask not just how far we can come to terms with and balance both intuitions, but also, far more generally, the extent to which we humans can understand one another, across cultures and even often within them, the limits, in other words, of mutual intelligibility. What commonalities can we detect in the matter of cognition across human beings whenever and wherever they have lived? Are the diversities such that there are impenetrable barriers to communication and understanding?

A brief introductory chapter examines where the problems originate, discusses some recent developments in those disciplines that have attempted to tackle them, identifies some of the major methodological pitfalls that lie in wait, and describes how and within what limits I hope—with my particular background and interests—to contribute to the clarification of the issues. I then turn to two studies that pick up points from anthropological and philosophical discussions of two general problems of interpretation. How should we cope with the diversity in the modes of discourse that are exemplified in our evidence and where can a study of the pragmatics of communication aid our interpretations? How do we react to what appear to be reports or records of gratuitously irrational behaviour? The first implicates the category of myth, the second that of magic, and my discussions aim to clear away some of the radical misunderstandings that those two topics have generated.

I turn next to two lines of argument that have been used to support the thesis of common, even universal, human cognitive capabilities, first the

Intelligence and Intelligibility: Cross-Cultural Studies of Human Cognitive Experience. G. E. R. Lloyd, Oxford University Press (2020). © G. E. R. Lloyd.
DOI: 10.1093/oso/9780198854593.001.0001

argument from language, then that from sociability. On the one hand, all humans possess language. Such an ability is not confined to humans among living creatures, but we can certainly undertake more complex acts of communication than are within the capabilities of other animals. But on the other hand, human languages are extremely diverse and we are all more or less aware, sometimes acutely so, of the difficulties of translating between them. Nor is the problem of understanding limited to translation across languages for it just as often arises within a single one.

Similarly where sociability is concerned, we are not the only living creatures to be social, but the societies we humans form and the modes of interaction we can engage in are more complex than anything in the animal kingdom as well as more diverse, and in many cases that has an impact on the ways in which one group judges another and attempts, or gives up the attempt, to achieve some understanding of those others.

After those wide-ranging forays, Chapter 6 turns the problem on its head. Instead of asking how mutual intelligibility is possible, I ask why it should ever fail. Can we pin down why it is sometimes so difficult to achieve a reasonable degree of mutual understanding? What light does the answer to that question throw on our cognitive abilities as a whole?

That will take me next to a review of what we learn from evolutionary studies both about what marks out humans from other species and also about the modes of differentiation within us humans.

The body of the investigation is then devoted to four areas of human experience that enable us to explore further commonalities and diversities. These four are 'mathematics', 'religion', 'law' and 'aesthetics'. In each case we start from a very provisional idea of what those areas comprise, as indicated by my using scare quotes for all four. But by the time we have brought to bear what we can learn from historical, ethnographic, philosophical and psychological studies, those initial concepts will need to be revised, and those revisions themselves bear on our recurrent problem of mutual understanding. We cannot afford to secure uniformity at the price of downplaying diversity. At the same time recognizing that difference should not lead us to lose sight of underlying commonalities.

A final chapter draws the threads of my discussion together, taking stock of the clarifications we have suggested, while recognizing the limitations of such successes as we can claim.

It remains to thank all my friends and colleagues at Cambridge, in the Needham Research Institute and the Faculties of Classics, History and Philosophy of Science, Social Anthropology, Philosophy and Asian and Middle Eastern Studies, who have helped me to formulate the arguments that I propose in this book, although it goes without saying that they cannot be held responsible for the ways I have used the advice they have given me. In the final stages I have benefited much from the extensive reports of three anonymous readers for OUP and for that and all his other oversight of the production of the book my thanks go to Peter Momtchiloff and his team.

G. E. R. L

1

Where Does the Problem Come from?

For an astonishing length of time most of those who lived in Europe assumed that, generally speaking, they had access to the truth, or if not the whole truth, at least to the methods to be used to attain that in the future. Yet many such assumptions had to contend first with the evident differences that separated different Europeans' views as to what precisely that truth consisted in, differences reflecting different religious beliefs and practices, political ideals, values, and ideas about how to behave correctly. Then that assumption also had to come to terms with the increasing knowledge of other civilizations. Some knowledge of Greco-Roman antiquity was common enough among members of the educated elite at least from the revival of learning in the thirteenth century onwards, but most of what was understood about other Mediterranean and Near Eastern societies was mediated by Greek or Latin authors, and although antiquity was admired by some for certain achievements, it was unfavourably contrasted with present times by those who stood for modernity. But as knowledge of India, China, Africa, the New World, came flooding into Europe, the challenges that posed to the original assumption of European superiority became increasingly difficult to ignore (Levitin 2015, 2019, Grafton 2019). How, in particular, was that knowledge to be squared with the teachings of the Bible? Were the people discovered in the Americas actually human?[1]

Even when their humanity was granted, the people of the New World were regularly despised as primitive, ignorant, stupid, childish, or all four. Their conversion to Christianity was a duty, and there was no

[1] When the conquistadors encountered native Americans in the Antilles, they wondered whether they were truly humans with souls that were there to be saved. The natives for their part worried whether the Spaniards had the same bodies as themselves. They drowned some of their Spanish prisoners to see if their bodies rotted. This story figures several times in discussions in Lévi-Strauss (1973: 76; 1976: ch. 18) and was taken up by Viveiros de Castro (1998: 475, 478–9; 2014: 50f.) among others (Descola 2013: 281, Latour 2009).

Intelligence and Intelligibility: Cross-Cultural Studies of Human Cognitive Experience. G. E. R. Lloyd, Oxford University Press (2020). © G. E. R. Lloyd.
DOI: 10.1093/oso/9780198854593.001.0001

compunction in appropriating their wealth or in turning them into slaves. It is true that, when confronting a complex literate society such as that of ancient China, Europeans could hardly be quite so dismissive. But the so-called rites controversy illustrates how Europeans still used Western categories in assessing everyone else (Gernet 1985). Did Chinese ancestor worship rate simply as customary ritual behaviour? In which case it could be tolerated. Or was it indeed a manifestation of a pagan religion? In which case Chinese Christian converts had to be forbidden to practise it. Clearly what passed as 'religion' was being judged by Western criteria, those provided by Christianity in particular. The idea that the category of the religious might be problematic was not seriously entertained, not at least by the adherents of the One True Faith, for that delivered certainty on the subject and ruled out any imposters.

Ethnography had its beginnings in justifications for Western colonialism or imperialism, even if it often provided the wherewithal to challenge the assumptions on which they were based. While, as we shall be considering in Chapter 3, Frazer, Malinowski, and Evans-Pritchard disagreed about so much, they all entertained the view that the beliefs and practices they labelled magic were rank superstition, failed science on one view, or failed technology on another, but on either a failure, for sure. Across the Channel, Lévy-Bruhl (1923) diagnosed a pre-logical mentality, that was based not on the Principle of Non-Contradiction, but on a Law of Participation. Stimulated by these and other developments a number of philosophers as well as ethnographers engaged in a fierce debate in the 1960s to the 1980s on what to make of so-called irrational beliefs (Wilson 1970, Horton and Finnegan 1973, Hollis and Lukes 1982, cf. Lukes 2000). Some protested that it was radically mistaken to use our notions of logic and science, indeed the basic concepts that underpin our world-view, to judge others' ideas. That often left unresolved the question of whether any understanding of another society is possible from outside that society itself. The extreme conclusion that was sometimes drawn was that it was only the members of a given society who were in any position to comprehend their belief system. The anthropologist had to go native to get anywhere near.[2]

---

[2] I discussed these debates in some detail in Lloyd 1990.

The debate about understanding other belief systems has certainly moved on in the last few decades and let me now take some time to outline some of the more important developments, even though unclarity persists on many points. The evident diversity in our thoughts still leads us to assume too readily that there *should be* some way of differentiating 'ways of thinking', even capacities of mind. Yet I remark on the differences in the expressions we use when we engage in such speculations. Some still believe that it is legitimate to speak of different 'mentalities' (or at least 'mentalités'), though I remain profoundly dissatisfied with any such notion (Lloyd 1990). How is a 'mentality' to be identified, and can a single individual have more than one of them, as some were led to claim with regard to complex historical figures (LeGoff 1974: 88 on Louis XI)? In general, 'mentalities' are at best a way of talking about what needs explaining, and when that is the case are no help whatsoever in their explanation.

Others prefer other locutions, 'mind-sets', 'casts of mind', 'character traits'. Of course we recognize different attitudes, habits, behaviour patterns, skills, dispositions, feelings, values between different individuals and within various groups. But the question is how far do any such differences provide the basis for a taxonomy of minds or of ways of thinking.

The issue continues to be much muddied by often blatantly racialist value judgements. It was part of Lévy-Bruhl's original project (1923, 1926, 1975) to diagnose what he called a 'pre-logical' mentality in primitive peoples, which on his view accounted for the mistakes they made. While he later came to abandon that idea of pre-logicality, he remained wedded to the idea of 'mentalités'. Similarly there was a famous set of studies by Luria (1976) based on his field-work in Siberia. He found many subjects who, he thought, were quite incapable of drawing the correct inferences from the premises with which they were supplied. In one group of studies, subjects were first told that in the Far North, where there is snow, all bears are white, and second, that Novaya Zemlya is in the Far North and that there is always snow there. They were then asked what colour the bears in Novaya Zemlya were. Some of those who replied said they did not know, as they had never been to Novaya Zemlya. One said: 'You've seen them: you know. I have never seen them, so how could I say?' (Luria 1976: 108–9, 112).

The inference Luria drew was that these individuals were deficient in the ability to reason logically and he put that down in part to their lack of formal schooling.[3] But instead of concluding that the subjects in question were weak logicians, the investigators might have inferred that they were brilliant pragmatists. When the investigator asked the question, 'What colour are the bears in Novaya Zemlya?', that implicitly threw doubt on the earlier information that in the Far North bears are white. Those who have been trained in syllogistic reasoning know that sequences of propositions are designed to test for validity, not for truth. But in ordinary conversational exchanges the interlocutors are interested in truth. From the pragmatist's point of view, the replies that Luria's interlocutors gave were both more honest and more intelligent. They were more honest, since they were in no position to pronounce on the colour of animals in a country they had never visited. And they were more intelligent, since they were responding to a conversational implicature.

Deficient logical skills have generally been diagnosed among indigenous predominantly oral groups. But a fair number of recent studies have revealed certain characteristic mistakes made also by the members of societies that pride themselves on their claimed status as advanced civilizations. The Wason test originated in 1966 (Wason 1966) and has since been studied in various guises. Originally the test went as follows. Subjects were presented with four cards where they were told that each card had a letter (A or B) on one side and a number (2 or 3) on the other, and then given the rule that if the letter is A the number is 2. Given four cards where the sides that could be seen carried A, B, 2, and 3 respectively, they were then asked which cards have to be turned over in order to *disprove* the rule. While most saw that the card showing A had to be turned over (for if it did not carry 2, the rule was disproved) few saw that the card with the number 3 also had to be. Instead they often chose the card with the number 2, where of course if the letter on the other side is an A, that *supports* the rule, though if the letter is a B that does not *disprove* it. Yet, interestingly, when the test was repeated where the cards carried realistic content, the subjects' score improved, even though that

---

[3] Yet whether the results have anything to do with schooling has been challenged; for example, by Dias, Roazzi and Harris 2005 (and cf. Mercier and Sperber 2017: 279ff.).

did not help those subjects much when the tests reverted to their more abstract form.[4]

The Wason test involves an ingenious experiment that does not, in its abstract form, figure as such in ordinary everyday life. But many other studies have explored kinds of reasoning that persist today that may in some cases go back deep into our evolutionary history, where there have been interestingly divergent conceptions of 'rationality' in play in their evaluation. Among the most prominent investigators tackling these questions from different angles have been Tversky and Kahneman (1974, cf. Kahneman and Tversky 1996), Fischhoff (1975), Tooby and Cosmides (1989), Evans (1989), Gigerenzer (1996, 2004), Tomasello (1999), Sternberg and Kaufman (2002), and Mercier and Sperber (2011). What our human ancestors in the Paleolithic needed was certainly not syllogistic nor any brand of formal logic, but rather what has been called 'fast and frugal' reasoning, where judgements have to be made with less than complete evidence, with less than total regard to all the information available, and more or less instantaneously. That is what humans and other animals need to be successful predators and to avoid being easy prey themselves. So this has spawned a series of studies investigating judgement under uncertainty which in turn have identified certain recurrent mistakes, notably the confirmation bias. As Fischhoff, for instance, showed (1975) (cf. Nickerson 1998), when people have been told the outcome of an event, they regularly overestimate the accuracy with which they would have predicted it if they had not been given such knowledge.

Yet while Kahneman and Tversky especially see 'fast and frugal' reasoning as flawed and subject to bias in a pejorative sense—in their view it fails to optimize utility and breaches the axioms of probability theory—Gigerenzer and his colleagues have insisted that in certain contexts and circumstances it can and does yield better—not just quicker and easier, but more accurate—results (see Gigerenzer and Goldstein 1996, Gigerenzer and Todd 1999, Gigerenzer and Brighton 2009). As Vranas (2000), Samuels, Stich, and Bishop (2002) and Sturm (2012)

---

[4] See Johnson-Laird, Legrenzi, and Legrenzi 1972. Among those who have appealed to pragmatic considerations to diagnose the source of what are represented as errors in carrying out the Wason test, Sperber, Cara, and Girotto 1995 have focused on the role of relevance in particular.

among others have pointed out, while both sides in this dispute are agreed that fast and frugal reasoning frequently occurs, the notions of rationality by which it is to be judged diverge. For Gigerenzer, to ignore certain parts of the data can be rational in the sense of efficient (he dubs this bounded or ecological rationality), while Kahneman (e.g. Kahneman and Tversky 1996) sticks with the traditional notion of logical rationality that depends on strict adherence to the norms of calculations of probability.

But where does that leave us on the question of the distribution of logical skills across populations? Mistakes from whatever cause (unexamined assumptions, overhasty conclusions, biases of many different types) are certainly not confined to particular human groups nor to whole societies, with or without high levels of literacy, with or without institutionalized schooling.[5] It is obvious that whether we engage in private reasoning to work out what to make of a situation or what to do for the best, or join with others in formal or informal discussion to exchange opinions on the problems, we are always fallible, both in evaluating what we see as the data and in judging what inferences that data necessitates or permits.

Of course it is not as if the self-conscious analysis of argumentation has no impact whatsoever. But the main effect may not lie in the improvement in the quality of the reasoning, for long after the formal analysis of argument began, fallacies were and still are being committed. The chief effect of making rules such as the Laws of Contradiction and Excluded Middle or such flaws as Petitio Principii or the Fallacy of the Consequent explicit is that they can then be *cited* to defeat, or at least to abash, opponents in the cut and thrust of debate. A sequence of arguments may, then, be criticized not just on the grounds of the truth or

---

[5] This is not to deny that literacy and educational institutionalization have an effect, as we shall be showing in subsequent studies. But the frequency of mistakes, even elementary ones, in every known society and at all periods does cast doubt on any view that would have it that literacy and institutions can be invoked to establish some Great Divide between human groups in the matter of their logicality even though theses of that general type have been so often proposed (Gellner 1973, Goody 1977, Havelock 1982, Ong 1982, Olson and Torrance 1991, Huff 2011). It is important too to recognize that an explicit concern to evaluate skills and flaws in arguing may be found in basically oral communities, as Gluckman (1965, 1967, 1972) showed in his studies of the Barotse.

appropriateness of the premises but also on the grounds that it breaches one or other logical rule.

However, it should be emphasized that the status of those laws and of other relevant concepts was and still is itself subject to debate. The commonest accusation in plenty of other societies besides the ancient Greeks is one of inconsistency. The ancient Chinese used the term *bei* to describe that and they delighted in stories of actual or imagined examples, as in that of the salesman who claimed first that his spears could penetrate any shield but then also that his shields could not be penetrated by anything whatsoever. But what counted as inconsistency was always subject to challenge (Lloyd 2018: 94–5). Some Greeks reacted to invocations of the Law of Contradiction by denying its truth or relevance, and nowadays we have not just three-value Logics but Paraconsistent ones (Priest, Routley, and Norman 1989, Priest 2008) claiming to be superior alternatives to the Classical variety. We may take differing views as to how successful those challenges are, but they certainly confirm the essential point, namely that the issues are still open to debate.

But if it can be claimed that we have in certain respects learnt how to avoid some of the grosser mistakes of our predecessors, it is certainly not the case that we are in a secure position to interpret the extraordinary diversity of human experience, of both beliefs and of practices, to which we nowadays have access. Indeed it is not just the substantive conclusions that we should draw that continue to be problematic: even the correct methods to work towards them, the rules of the game, continue to be disputed, both across different academic disciplines (anthropology, philosophy, history of science, psychology, cognitive science) and even within them.

I set myself the task, in this book, of contributing to the clarification of some of the basic issues. How can we set about understanding others? That includes first how we should evaluate their cognitive capacities, their intelligence, and second, understanding what they thought there is to be understood. The recurrent difficulty we face is that if we simply apply our own conceptual schemata in our inquiries, is that not bound to distort our interpretations? But how can we adapt and revise those schemata to make them fit for purpose? The hope is that a close scrutiny of the diverse data available to us will enable us not only to make better sense of that data, but to learn where our own initial assumptions need to be overhauled.

I should, however, explain my own background and how I got into these debates, for that will help to pinpoint the limitations of what I can hope to contribute. Trained initially as a Classicist, I was introduced early on to two conflicting views of the Greek experience, one that held it up as a model to be followed, with covert undertones of the Glory that was Greece, if not of the Greek miracle. But an alternative understanding, pioneered especially by E.R. Dodds (1951), put the emphasis on the elements of the Irrational in Greek culture. For some, the Greeks could be appealed to not just as great innovative geniuses, but as the founders of both philosophy and science (even though they had no concept that corresponds precisely to the latter). For others, the great virtue of studying their culture was that it introduced us to a challengingly alien society. Dodds' own forays into what were at the time fashionable anthropological ideas, shamanism, for instance, and the contrast between shame culture and guilt culture, were pretty disastrous. But the lesson I took away from my reading of his work was that it was possible, within certain limits, to treat the study of the Greeks as a kind of ancient anthropology.

A visit to China in 1987 taught me how important it was to learn classical Chinese to make the most of the very considerable possibilities for comparing and contrasting these two great ancient civilizations. Such a comparative study poses its own special problems. As in anthropology we must always locate the evidence we have against the background of the group or society from which it originates, guarding against the danger of taking outliers as in some way typical of the community as a whole, and of course with antiquity we are in no position to revisit our sources to interview our informants to check the viability of our interpretations. At the same time the particular advantage of studying these two ancient civilizations is that they both provide access to some sophisticated, self-conscious discussions of the key problems of the nature of intelligence and the conditions of intelligibility with which I am concerned.

On the one hand, then, I aim to make the most of literate sources that approach the problems with conceptual frameworks that differ markedly from those we are used to in later Western modernity. On the other, my collaborations with anthropologists, historians and philosophers of science, cognitive scientists and others serve as reminders of how the central issues of understanding others and the worlds they understood surface in many other modalities in other disciplines. Obviously in such areas as empirical studies of children's psychological development, the cognitive capacities of non-human animals, the investigation of human emotions by way of fMRI scans, I am in no position to engage directly. Nor am I qualified to pronounce authoritatively on the claims and counterclaims made nowadays concerning the artificial intelligence of computers.[6] But even an observer on the sidelines, such as myself, can offer some observations on the relevance of such studies to the strategic questions of the nature of understanding and intelligence, of the possibilities, difficulties and limitations of intelligibility, and of the character of what there is to be understood. It is in that spirit and with these reservations that I tackle here the major problems posed by those issues. If it is apparent that neither I nor anyone else occupies a privileged position to adjudicate on the matter, the question of what we can learn from the exploration is eminently worth pursuing. Or so I would maintain.

---

[6] There is a fine preliminary exploration of the state of the question in McCarty 2019. Obviously computers are not social beings and so lack the kinds of intelligence we can discern in human social, moral, and cultural behaviour and interactions. As for my second argument based on language, that of computers is constrained by the demands of absolute explicitness and complete consistency and so cannot cope with the semantic stretch that I see as so important in our discourse. Nevertheless if we allow, as we surely must, that different modes of intelligence are in play in planning, calculating, inferring, deciding, puzzle-solving, working out causes, and understanding others, we should recognize the capabilities of computers in some of these activities and conclude that they exhibit a distinctive mode of intelligence rather than no intelligence at all. Recent studies of their performance in games of Go (Alpha Go Zero) show that computers can learn simply from repeated playing against themselves without human instruction beyond that involved in the initial information concerning the rules of the game, and indeed that their subsequent performance sometimes outstrips that of the most accomplished human experts. We should however note that this is in a determinate environment where, precisely, the rules and aims of the exercise are fixed and immutable. The jury is still out on the extent to which computers currently do, or in the future will, show analogous capacities to learn in other more open-ended situations.

2

Modes of Discourse and the Pragmatics of Communication

The interpretation of the statements reported in the ethnographic record or in ancient texts has often been unduly influenced by the assumption or the expectation that they contain declarative utterances that imply or express theories or explanations that should be evaluated simply by the criteria of truth and falsity. One might have thought that any such assumptions would have been exposed as the drastic oversimplifications they are by two developments in the philosophy of language that go back to the 1960s. First there was J.L. Austin's distinction between various types of speech acts, first identifying performatives, and then drawing further distinctions between locutionary, illocutionary, and perlocutionary utterances.[1] Then there was Grice's introduction of the notion of conversational implicature and the distinction he drew between word meaning, sentence meaning, and utterer's meaning.[2] In practice, however, although the anthropologist Tambiah (1968, 1973, 1985, 1990) made notable use of Austin, these ideas did not have the penetration outside the field of philosophy of language itself that one might have hoped.

But if we are to do justice to the complexity and the variety in the force of different speech acts, and to the significance that should have on how we understand them, we need to go way beyond the original perceptions of Austin and Grice. Two tricky interrelated topics are the degree of

---

[1] Austin defined 'performatives' as those utterances that are or are part of the doing of an action, as in 'I name this ship the *Queen Elizabeth*' (Austin 1962: 5), and he went on to distinguish locutionary speech acts in general as the performance of an utterance first from illocutionary ones where the statement has pragmatic force and then from perlocutionary ones that relate to the causal effect of the utterance on the addressee.

[2] Grice introduced these distinctions in 1968 and followed them up in his 1975, 1978, and 1989.

Intelligence and Intelligibility: Cross-Cultural Studies of Human Cognitive Experience. G. E. R. Lloyd, Oxford University Press (2020). © G. E. R. Lloyd.
DOI: 10.1093/oso/9780198854593.001.0001

seriousness or playfulness of statements,[3] and the differences that different interlocutors or audiences may make.

Obviously the seriousness of a speech act in the formal setting of a court of law or of an audience with a king or person in authority differs from the light-heartedness with which riddles are propounded for entertainment or stories are told to keep the children quiet. Yet the issue may not be as straightforward as that. Aristotle already reports in the *Rhetoric* (1419b3ff.) that the sophist Gorgias suggested as a rhetorical gambit that you destroy your opponent's seriousness with laughter and his laughter with your seriousness. Other sophists such as Euthydemus and Dionysodorus are criticized in Plato's dialogues for indulging in logic-chopping rather than getting on with the important business of educating the young. Yet getting the young to pay due attention to their instructors is recognized to be difficult even when those teachers are doing their best to achieve that end (Plato, *Republic* 539b).

But if many ancient writers, Greek, Chinese, and Indian, show an awareness of the issue of speakers' intentions, the problem for us, as interpreters of ancient texts, is that the accounts we are given of the contexts of communication are often simply not rich and detailed enough for us to gauge the tone of the exchanges. Even with much fuller evidence we have to allow for the possibility of speakers being deliberately opaque, allowing them to claim, if need be, that they have been misunderstood. Paradox and riddles may be used to shake people out of their common assumptions or they may be designed merely to tease, but we may often be at a loss to say which or what was originally intended.

These simple points are clearly relevant to many of the problems of interpretation raised in those disputes over apparently irrational beliefs that I have mentioned. I shall shortly be considering the vocabulary available to different indigenous groups to indicate differences in modes of discourse. But certainly we should not ignore the question of the nature of the commitment entered into in the assertions that outsiders are likely to find to be counter-intuitive.

---

[3] The theme of the playful or the ludic in different contexts and modes of discourse has been explored by Huizinga (1970) and Caillois (1961) especially. In his *Ludic Proof*, Netz (2009) points to the ludic elements in Hellenistic culture, not least in the mathematics of the period. At the opposite end of the spectrum, words themselves may be thought to have magical power when, for example, they are invoked in spells or other rituals (Tambiah 1968).

The second topic I mentioned was the role of audiences. You may, at one end of the spectrum, be giving free rein to your imagination to amuse the children, or at the other, be hoping to impress a ruler, a minister, a judge, someone on whom your career, your livelihood, even your life may depend. A speaker's tactics may differ according to whether they are addressing experts or a lay audience, and depending on whether a rival is waiting in the wings, ready to make alternative proposals. In such a competitive situation the speaker may spend more time demolishing their opponents' case than in trying to give good arguments to establish their own. There is then the further delicate matter of the extent to which the authority of those who will be adjudicating the debate should or can be challenged. In this context there are obvious risks that any such move may do nothing to undermine the judges, but merely antagonize them.

We have good evidence in extant texts from ancient Greece, China, and India that throws light on the variety of debating situations that persuaders might face. In Greece exhibition speeches, called *epideixeis*, were sometimes held in front of a lay audience. Even though the subject-matter debated could include such speculative topics as the component elements of the human body or of the cosmos as a whole, it was the audience itself who decided who among the rival speakers had won the argument (cf. the Hippocratic treatise *On the Nature of Man*). In ancient China by contrast in the debates held on such matters as the regulation of the calendar the ultimate decision rested with kings, or after the unification the Emperor or his representatives, and the participants were aware that advocating a proposal that displeased them could lead to disgrace, punishment, even death (Cullen 2007).

Ancient India in turn provides a third model (Matilal 1985, Mohanty 1992, Prets 2000, 2001, Bronkhorst 2007). The *Upaniṣads* present a picture of debates between gurus on some highly abstruse topics, the number of gods, for instance, or the nature of *brahman*. But here it is the gurus themselves who decide who has won. Victory depends on posing a question to which your rival has no answer. You are not supposed to ask a question to which you yourself do not know the correct answer. When your opponent is stumped and falls silent, that is an admission of defeat, and that in turn can lead, as Bronkhorst (2002) showed, to the abject humiliation of the loser, who is forced to act as the servant of the winner.

It is striking that while Greek and Chinese texts recognize inconsistency as a flaw in argument, the gurus in the Indian texts have no compunction in offering what seem to us quite contradictory answers to the same question.[4]

This, then, takes me to the important issue of the extent to which the actors themselves have a vocabulary to describe the formal characteristics of different modes of discourse, where the first point to note is that it is not just literate societies that have a rich set of terms to describe the virtues and vices of arguments and arguers. As we noted before (Chapter 1, note 5), the Barotse studied by Gluckman when they were still a predominantly oral society were one whose members prided themselves on their connoisseurship in that domain.

One topic that has attracted a particular amount of attention is whether a given society recognizes what we call its myths as such, although it should be immediately obvious that the prior question should be whether any such category is applicable or appropriate. Our term is derived, of course, from the Greek *muthos* and much has been written about some supposed development, in Greek thought, from myth to what is sometimes its antonym, namely *logos*. Yet as has been repeatedly pointed out (Buxton 1999, Calame 1999) neither term in that pairing is univocal. The range of *logos* includes word, speech, ratio as well as rational account. *Muthos* sometimes carries the negative associations of fictional account, where it is appropriate to suspend belief in its truth, but it can also sometimes be used interchangeably with *logos*, as indeed is the case in Plato when he describes the cosmological story in the *Timaeus* both as an *eikōs logos* and as an *eikōs muthos*. Yet of course elsewhere Plato is as keen as any philosopher to draw distinctions between accounts that claim to be true and those that do not.

In many groups the key contrast is not between truth and fiction but rather between what a person can vouch for on the basis of their personal experience and what they cannot—though that may include what they accept on the basis of someone else's report. This is a distinction to be found in different versions in the Greek historians from Herodotus if not

---

[4] Questioned on the number of gods, the sage Yājñavalkya gives seven different answers each with its own justification, each accepted by his interlocutor, who nevertheless persists each time in questioning him further: 'Yes, of course, but really, Yājñavalkya, how many gods are there?' *Bṛhadāraṇyaka Upaniṣad* 3.9, Olivelle 1996: 46–7, Lloyd 2014: 31.

from Homer himself onwards (Hartog 1988, Thomas 2002), in the Chinese Mohists,[5] and in the indigenous peoples reported on by Luria (though as we noted before he was so critical of their logical abilities). In some languages there are distinctive grammatical ways in which the different bases for a claim are differentiated, as has been discussed under the rubric of evidentiality since Aikhenvald 2004.

A more complex set of discriminations is recorded for the Barasana in north-west Amazonia by Stephen Hugh-Jones.

> The Barasana category *bukūra keti* ['old people's stories'] is normally applied to narrated myth but can also be used to refer to other historical narratives, to genealogies and to stories about the deeds of previous generations and past clan ancestors. At the other extreme the word *basa* covers song, dance and instrumental music. The category *keti oka*, which might be translated as 'sacred, powerful speech, thought or esoteric knowledge' applies, in particular, to ritual chants . . . But in a more extended sense *keti oka* applies not only to chants and shamanic spells, but also to dance songs, to the songs latent in the melodies of Yurupari flutes, and also to ritual objects, petroglyphs and sacred sites.
>
> (Hugh-Jones 2016: 160)

Obviously these distinctions do not map at all straightforwardly on to our general contrast between myth as fiction versus rational account. But it would be absurd to criticize the Barasana categories as flawed on those grounds. Rather we must first take on board that they find other distinctions relevant to an analysis of modes of discourse and second, bear this in mind when we are faced with the problem of understanding their stories, ritual speech acts, spells and so on. Once again the basic lesson we should take away from this is that the statements attributed to the

---

[5] While the teachings associated with Mozi were perceived as the main rivals to those associated with Confucius in the Warring States period, that is before the unification of China accomplished by Qin Shi Huang Di in 221 BCE, they were later eclipsed when the latter came to form the core of the curriculum of the Chinese imperial Academy. So the interpretation of the fragmentary extant Mohist sources continues to be much disputed, see Graham 1978, Johnston 2010. We do, however, have good evidence that they discussed the bases and justification for claims to know in several contexts, where they distinguished beliefs guaranteed by direct observation from those based on the reports of others or on the authority of the sage kings. See *Mozi* 31 and 35 especially, Graham 1989: 36ff., Johnston 2010: 288, 318ff.

Barasana do not all carry the same valence, the same kind and degree of commitment.

The interest of this material lies not only and not especially in the question mark it raises concerning whether 'myth', however understood, is a valid cross-cultural category. The more general point is that the actors' own categories of modes of discourse have always to be borne in mind when evaluating whatever ideas or beliefs are ascribed to them and indeed the implications of their practices and modes of behaviour. Not everything they say or do should be treated on a par with their most mundane communications and everyday activities.

To take a well-known example from the debates I mentioned in Chapter 1, we are told by the ethnographers that the Dorze believe that the leopard is a Christian animal (Sperber 1975, 1980, 1985, 1997). Much ink has been spilt over whether this is intended literally or merely figuratively though the question of whether the Dorze make any such kind of distinction is generally not addressed. But pressing that contrast poses a dilemma. On the literal reading, the Dorze were either mistaken or they had some alternative way of assessing truth or falsehood to which we have no access. Or if such a statement is to be taken figuratively or symbolically, and the Dorze are not committed to the strict belief that the leopard is Christian, at least we are owed an account of the respects it is like a Christian or not. The ethnography provides some help on that subject, but is short on the detail that we need to assess the context of the communicative exchange in which such a statement would occur. In the view I am advocating here, it is the quality of that communicative exchange that would provide the key to a better understanding of the statement.

Meanwhile, it is worth bearing in mind that there is no shortage of highly counter-intuitive belief statements with which we are familiar in our own society. We appreciate that asserting that God is one and that He is three is to express allegiance to a complex set of beliefs, the strangeness of which serves, among other things, to mark out their importance. Suspending disbelief in the apparent contradiction is, for the faithful, a necessary condition for progress in true understanding. I am not saying we are in a position to say precisely how we should comprehend the Dorze point of view. But the resources to do so must include an appreciation of their sense of the variety of the modes of discourse in which they engage.

A focus on the categories of modes of discourse, such as I am advocating, does not have as its aim to make every statement we find in the ethnographic or historical records come out true—which would be some grotesque exaggeration of Davidson's principle of charity in interpretation (Davidson 2001). Rather it is to cast doubt on whether many of the statements in question are candidates for truth or falsehood in the first place. That leaves open, of course, just how the statements are intended and for that we have to make the best use we can of what we know about the varieties of communicative act the actors explicitly or implicitly recognize. Those we have been used to, in the West, may sometimes provide a useful enough framework, but may prove to be, in the respects I have indicated, seriously misleading.

My main argument has been to point to the dangers of applying common Western categories to the interpretation of much of what is reported in the ethnographic and historical records. The contrasts between the literal and the metaphorical, and between myth and rational account, turn out often to be inapplicable and even misleading. That is not just because the actors themselves, whom we are studying, generally had no equivalent categories, but also because those contrasts force issues and raise false expectations about the criteria that proper statements of beliefs should meet. We look for well-formed formulae but forget how rare these are in our own discourse when we are not actually doing logic. The anthropologist and the historian should be wary of our categories even if this leaves them with the more difficult task of exploring, on each occasion, the actors' own assumptions concerning modes of discourse and the nature of the communicative exchanges in which they participate.

3

Magic

Efficacy and Felicity

The first people whom we know to have forged an explicit category of 'magic' to describe certain behaviour patterns and speech acts were (once again) certain ancient Greeks. The consequences of this move for the issue of how others are to be understood would be hard to overestimate, for it provided a deadly weapon of polemic to denigrate large swathes both of others' beliefs and of their practices. The history of the development of the term *mageia* (or *magiē*) has often been written.[1] The two crucial points relevant for our immediate concerns here are first the association with foreigners—*mageia* itself is derived from Magoi, a group of Persians or else a set of their priests—and second and relatedly the strongly negative undertones with which it was invested. This is especially the case in the Hippocratic treatise *On the Sacred Disease*, the author of which attacks his opponents by comparing them to Magoi. They held that the sacred disease (according to his rather detailed description, a type of what we would call Grand Mal epilepsy) is indeed sacred, caused by gods or demons, to be treated by purifications, spells, and incantations. But they are no better than charlatans and quacks, their treatments worthless rubbish.

It is important to notice that this author mounts a complex attack on several fronts, including accusing his rivals of positive impiety for their claiming that they could control the gods. They are mercenary exploiters of their unfortunate patients. They are ignorant and their ways of treating the disease, their 'purifications', are quite ineffective. They claim to know which god or demon is responsible for which type of the disease,

---

[1] See, for example, Faraone and Obbink 1991 and Graf 1999, especially with references to many earlier studies and cf. Faraone 1999, Collins 2008, Martin 2012.

Intelligence and Intelligibility: Cross-Cultural Studies of Human Cognitive Experience. G. E. R. Lloyd, Oxford University Press (2020). © G. E. R. Lloyd.
DOI: 10.1093/oso/9780198854593.001.0001

but that is to mask their complete ignorance of the cause of the disease, which, according to the Hippocratic author, is, like every other disease, a natural one. In fact he offers a specific account, saying that it arises from the blocking of the veins or vessels in the brain. The cause of this blockage is phlegm and he even offers a differential diagnosis, saying that the disease attacks the phlegmatic more than the bilious. The charms and purifications his opponents rely on do no good at all. They are simply the means whereby the purifiers con their gullible clients, making a lot of money out of them in the process.

Now this is not an ethnographic report so much as a piece of particularly aggressive medical polemic. But it is extraordinary how influential this original attack on 'magic' came to be in both history of science and anthropology. Even when there were opportunities to follow up ethnographic reports, what was labelled 'magic' was *ipso facto* dismissed as botched science or botched technology, based on superstition. The primitive peoples who engaged in such could not be expected to have any real idea of causes and effects, nor any inkling of the True Religion. If occasionally it was noticed that a certain similarity could be found between human sacrifice and Christ's crucifixion, and between cannibalism and Holy Communion, the pagan versions were to be dismissed as macabre, diabolical perversions of the true Sacraments. The latter had the Church, the priesthood, the Bible as their guarantors, while primitive people wallowed in false belief from which it was the duty of civilized people to rescue them.

Such a picture is only a slight caricature when we think of the ways in which such influential figures as Frazer went about constructing a view of the contrasts between Magic, Science, and Religion. It was not just the armchair scholar, Frazer, but one of the founders of empirical ethnography, Malinowski, who, writing an article with precisely that title in 1925, defined magic in contrast, on the one hand, to science, and on the other to religion. Echoes of those distinctions persist in the next generation of anthropologists. Evans-Pritchard's pioneering *Witchcraft, Oracles and Magic among the Azande* (1937) offered a tripartite distinction between 'mystical notions', 'common-sense notions', and 'scientific notions', where the mystical is still defined negatively. These are 'patterns of thought that attribute to phenomena supra-sensible qualities which, or part of which, are not derived from observation or cannot be inferred from it, and which they do not possess' (1937: 12). But a couple of decades later something of a reaction set in, including among Evans-Pritchard's most ardent followers. Thus Mary Douglas had some caustic remarks to make about what she saw as naive interpretations of !Kung Bushmen rituals when in *Purity and Danger* (1966: 79) she wrote:

> Once when a band of !Kung Bushmen had performed their rain rituals, a small cloud appeared on the horizon, grew and darkened. Then rain fell. But the anthropologists who asked if the Bushmen reckoned the rite had produced the rain, were laughed out of court.

Douglas was here drawing on a report by Lorna Marshall (1957), but Marshall's own view is more complex than Douglas allows it to appear. Marshall does describe how she was intent on a particularly fine performance of the rain dance and did not notice that 'the first storm of the season had crept up behind us and suddenly burst over us like a bomb'. She then asked one of her informants if he believed that the dance had brought the rain, to which he replied that 'the rain was due to come. The dance had not brought it' (Marshall 1957: 238). Yet elsewhere in the same article, Marshall reports that the aim of the rain dance was to cure the sick and that the Bushmen performed other rituals, for example, cutting the throats of certain animals, that were designed to bring or stop rain (Marshall 1957: 237, 239).

But if in certain quarters blanket dismissals of magic as sheer stupidity were replaced by some overoptimistic rationalizations, it was above all Tambiah, who, in a series of articles in 1968, 1973, and then in his Morgan lectures (1990) proposed a different taxonomy of the possible goals of magical beliefs and practices. We should distinguish those that aim at causal efficacy on the one hand, and those that target felicity or appropriateness on the other. As noticed before, Tambiah was here drawing on Austin's 1962 discussion of *How to Do Things with Words*, while we also find him hesitating about just how far his taxonomy was able to provide a general account of magic—a reservation that can be strengthened by recalling the point I made in Chapter 2, namely that it is far from always the case that any given society will have a category that corresponds to 'magic' in the first place.

Yet we must certainly bear in mind the efficacy/felicity distinction when we approach the interpretation of the diverse data provided by anthropology, by history, and even by reflection on our own contemporary society. Applying the distinction opens up several different ways in which an action can succeed or fail. It can plausibly be assumed that there is no group or individual that has no concept of the possibility of error. But that may be a matter of fact—a mistake in perception or inference or calculation, for instance—or it may be that the fault lies in the incorrect performance of an act, where there is no question of the action being false, just that it was inappropriate. That may be because the performers lacked the necessary skill or knowledge or even had been incorrectly instructed by those who were supposed to be in control of the rituals or ceremonies.

An examination of what types of error get most attention can throw considerable light on the values of the groups in question. Let me turn back to the ancient Greek data to see the relevance of the efficacy/felicity distinction there. We noticed the exceptionally aggressive attack, in *On the Sacred Disease*, on the purifiers who claim to treat that complaint but who—the Hippocratic author states—do not know what they are talking about. He uses the category of 'magic' to drive a wedge between his naturalistic account and the superstitious nonsense of his rivals (*deisidaimonia* is his word for 'superstition'). But of course we do not now know what they might have said in self-defence. For some ideas about that, we may turn to the evidence for an admittedly rather different, certainly more established, mode of religious healing, namely that practised in the shrines of healing gods or heroes such as Apollo and Asclepius.

The inscriptions set up outside many of those shrines show how temple medicine presented itself to its clientele.[2] Those who came to consult the god suffered from a wide variety of illnesses and misfortunes, including the loss of a child or precious property. In every single case that

---

[2] Our main fifth- and fourth-century BCE evidence comes from Epidaurus, though there were healing shrines in many other cities in the Greek and then the Roman world, including Athens, Cos, Pergamum, and Rome itself. See Herzog 1931, Edelstein and Edelstein 1945, LiDonnici 1995. I discussed the rivalry between what I called secularization and sacralization in Lloyd 2003: ch. 3, where I point out the contemporary development of both trends and the continued existence of both to the end of pagan antiquity.

is extant from Epidaurus the outcome is a success, though sometimes there is some delay in this, as the patient is represented as having to overcome an initial scepticism or indeed a reluctance to pay the dues the god demanded. Sometimes the cure is effected by the god offering advice or by administering drugs. But sometimes the god is described as intervening directly, for example by performing surgical operations. This may be said to be what the patient dreams. But on occasion the report purports to describe what happened while the patient was wide awake, in front of eyewitnesses who would be in a position to vouch for the truth of the account, however extravagant. In one case the god cuts the patient's head off, removes the parasites that are the cause of the infection, and then sews the head back on again.[3]

Several points are important in this material. First the main object of the inscriptions is, of course, propaganda, to spread the word concerning the powers of the god and to inspire confidence in the patients and their carers that they can enlist his help. Thus far the effect is psychological. But the patients were not just out for solace: they wanted a cure for their ills, even though what counted as a cure was open to interpretation, as indeed was what counted as an illness or disease. However, when they came to consult about a lost child, it would only be the restoration of the child that would be a satisfactory outcome. In view of this, it would clearly be quite wrong to suggest that these ancient healers were fighting their battles and defending their reputations purely under the banner of felicity or appropriateness. Their counter-attack to the naturalists' claims to causal efficacy was based on counter-claims of superior causal efficacy—and, in judging that, we should bear in mind just how speculative the accounts of the disease were in *On the Sacred Disease* and how exaggerated were its claims that this complaint, like every other, could be cured by controlling regimen, provided that the right moment was chosen.[4]

---

[3] This is case 23 on Epidaurus Stele B (LiDonnici 1995: B 3): see Lloyd 2003: 76f.

[4] Although at one point the Hippocratic writer refers to what would be found if one opened the skull of a goat suffering from the disease—to support his claim that there is a natural cause at work—he nowhere contemplates following up his own explanation that the complaint arises from the blocking of the veins in the head nor does he offer any account of their anatomy. As for his claim that the disease is curable, he writes in his final chapter: 'A man with the knowledge of how to produce, by regimen, dryness and moisture, cold and heat in the human body, could

Whereas an earlier positivist historiography of medical science supposed that the advent of naturalistic medicine would spell the end of religious therapy, that is clearly not borne out by the facts. Temple medicine continued to flourish in the Greco-Roman world until the end of pagan antiquity and was even transformed after the Christian takeover, when healing saints, and Christ Himself, took over the roles previously played by Apollo and Asclepius (Nutton 1988: ch. 10; Lloyd 2003: ch. 8). Nor would it be correct to argue that adherence to religious medicine was confined to the uneducated masses. Some members of the literate elite, such as the orator Aelius Aristides (second century CE) were enthusiastic followers, explicitly preferring to put their trust in Asclepius (and his representatives) rather than in ordinary doctors.

Some of this can be put down to the striking fact that many of the doctors represented in the Hippocratic Corpus honestly confess that they were at a loss as to how to cure or even alleviate many of the severe conditions their patients suffered from, the deaths of many of whom they do not hesitate to record. At the same time we should not suppose that ancient patients were making their decisions about whom to consult purely on the basis of claimed or perceived causal efficacy, for that would be to leave out of account that sometimes considerations of felicity were in play. This would be the case, for example, when they entertained expectations to do with the appropriateness of following traditional patterns of behaviour designed to enlist the help of the gods.

Much more could be said about the competing styles of justification available in the Greco-Roman world, but it is time now to turn to our second great ancient civilization to review the situation there, while acknowledging, first of all, that it is as foolhardy to attempt to generalize across groups and periods in China as it is about Greece. It is, however, fair to notice that there is less interest in attempts to provide causal explanations of most natural phenomena (as we call them) than there is in early Greek thought. In the fourth century BCE there is one notable individual who went in for such in a big way, namely Hui Shi, who is reported as attempting to say why the earth did not fall or what caused

cure this disease too, provided he could distinguish the right moment for the application of what is beneficial, without recourse to purifications and magic.'

wind, rain, thunder, or the like. Yet all he got for his pains was mockery for the fatuity of his efforts and criticism for wasting his talents (*Zhuangzi* 33: 80–7).[5] But where disease was concerned, there were general accounts, indeed—as in Greece—divergent ones, proposed by rival groups of healers.

There was no equivalent, in China, of the impressively well-established shrines to Asclepius in ancient Greece. But among the competing groups of healers there were those whose discourse focused on neutralizing the effects of invasive demons or evil spirits. Some of these were those called *wu*, mediums, who went in for exorcisms and were also reputed to be able to control the weather, bringing or stopping rain. But other practitioners argued that the chief causes of diseases were invasive physical factors, heteropathic *qi*, or other influences that upset the balance within the body. As in ancient Greece, Chinese healers of all kinds were generally at a loss to treat acute diseases, but offered varying combinations of psychological support, herbal and more specialized remedies, acupuncture, and moxibustion (Harper 1998). Many conditions were put down to excesses in the matter of food, drink, and sex,[6] and Chinese doctors were not short of good advice about avoiding these.

Correct behaviour in general meant performing the rituals deemed appropriate for different occasions. This theme figures large in the extant texts associated with Confucius and other members of the literate elite, the *ru*, though not all of those agreed with what they represented Confucius as teaching. Good manners, proper deportment, the meticulous observance of rituals both at home and at court were all part of what made an individual a proper gentleman, *junzi*. These were not matters where the causal efficacy of behaviour was in question: rather they were judged by their appropriateness and felicity. However, that certainly did not mean that everyone was in agreement about how this was to be achieved, even though the right answer to that was not to be judged by concrete results. To be sure, we are now often reduced to mere guesswork

---

[5] The *Zhuangzi* is a collection of texts dating from between the fourth and the second century BCE associated with Zhuang Zhou: see Graham 1981.

[6] This is a recurrent motif in the case histories recorded in the biography of the second-century BCE physician Chunyu Yi in the first great dynastic history, the *Shiji*, composed by Sima Tan and his son Sima Qian around 100 BCE. See Hsu 2010.

in our efforts to understand why some practice or behaviour was favoured over others. Justification in terms of some notion of what had the sanction of tradition is common, but that just pushes the question one stage further back. Nor are we any clearer as to the reasons why some self-styled experts on court etiquette came to gain that reputation.

But if much remains obscure, one recurrent claim does stand out, namely that the acid test for good advice was what secured good government and avoided disorder, *luan*, however that was conceived (Lloyd 2010). In just about every intellectual domain, including in several we would classify as philosophy or science, the goal was to advise the ruler on how to govern well, even though the connection between particular counsel and that end result was often thoroughly disputed. The focus on deportment, ritual behaviour and other aspects of felicity does point to a contrast between some Chinese and some Greek thinkers. As we saw, Greek 'naturalistic' medical writers attacked their rivals on the grounds that they were ignorant of the causes of diseases and of how they should be treated, a matter, then, of causal efficacy in those naturalists' views. But when Confucius is represented as being asked for his views on such matters as marvels, prodigies, ghosts, or demons (topics on which the Mohists argued at length in favour of adopting traditional views)[7] he replies that he does not talk about such issues (*Lunyu* 7.21, cf. 6.22 and 3.12).[8] What he is concerned with, as he constantly emphasizes, is human virtue (humaneness, *ren* 仁) and good government. Confucius refuses to be drawn on the question of whether the dead have knowledge, as being the wrong type of preoccupation from the point of view of what is important for life.

What is at stake is the primary values of each society, or of groups within it. It would clearly be absurd to represent all Greeks as taking the view of the naturalists represented in the Hippocratic Corpus or in Greek philosophy, just as it would be to generalize to all Chinese on the basis of what we find attributed to Confucius in the *Lunyu*. But at a different level a contrast can be found in the different positions occupied by influential

---

[7] This is the topic of *Mozi* 31 especially: see Johnston 2010: 278ff.

[8] The *Lunyu* used to be ascribed to Confucius himself, but is now recognized to be an amalgam of texts compiled over an extended period of time by those who considered themselves his followers.

writers in our two ancient societies and this is indirectly relevant to the distinction I have drawn between efficacy and felicity. Most Chinese intellectuals were clear, as we said, that their primary responsibility was to offer wise advice to the ruler on good government. Those intellectuals often occupied positions at court and some were responsible for teaching in the Academies that trained those who went on to posts in the Chinese civil service. In Greece the institutions of higher education (as we may call them) were private and although they were frequented by plenty of individuals who went on to political careers, that was their choice, not the fulfilment of a state-sponsored programme. The Greek ideal of individual happiness certainly did not exclude a concern for politics, but that was not the primary focus. From an ancient Chinese point of view much of what the Greeks included in the inquiry into nature was irrelevant speculation.

It may seem that our discussion has strayed unduly far from the topic of magic with which we began. But it can be argued that the distinction between efficacy and felicity that we have drawn is relevant to the way in which magic itself came to be the focus of explicit polemic. This happened in the context we have described in ancient Greece where in certain circles at least it was turned into a term of abuse. Yet that move depended, in large part, on the battle between competing views being represented as a matter of which gave the correct causal account. Magic is nonsense (according to the naturalists) because it locates the causes at work in the wrong place, as a matter of divine intervention, not of physical interaction. While the traditionalists certainly claimed that their reference to the gods showed true piety, they implicitly accepted, at least up to a point, the naturalists' argument that appealed to results, in the case of temple medicine, of actual cures.

It is not that there is no concern for causal efficacy in China, of course. Yet causal explanations of physical phenomena generally take second place to a focus on what contributes to good government, a very different way in which advice could be judged to be of practical utility. While there is, as we have seen, plenty of controversy and dispute on all sorts of topics among Chinese thinkers, the boundary between different types of justification for their styles of advice was less sharply drawn and they tended to agree that the prime goal was to secure the welfare of 'all under heaven'. The *wu* were often marginalized and feared, and superstitious traditions were criticized as mistaken and wasteful.[9] But the disputes did not proceed by way of the invocation of a concept that prejudged the issues in favour of those who claimed to have the correct kind of causal explanations, one that avoided committing a category mistake by offering supernatural accounts of natural phenomena.

None of this is to suggest that 'magic' is such a confused and confusing term that it has no place in our analysis. But it is to underline some of the difficulties in its use. Does it correspond to an actors' category, in which case what is it contrasted with? Or is it just an observers' category where again how that applies to the original data must be scrutinized? It is particularly where 'magic', however construed, is contrasted with 'science' or with 'rational account' that we must beware, for we have to bear in mind that 'magical' statements and practices may not have causal efficacy, but felicity, as their goal. When that is the case it should not be a question of pronouncing on their truth or falsity, but one of determining their appropriateness. The upshot is that much of the discussion of this topic in ethnography and history has been at cross-purposes, underestimating the different ways in which success and failure can be judged. This is not to say that mistakes never happen or were never recognized by the actors themselves. But rather that attention needs to be paid to the register in which they occur, and correspondingly to the expectations and values of the group concerned. Once again, as in Chapter 2, we find that hasty assumptions about what is being attempted whether in action or in words may act as an impediment to our understanding.

---

[9] This is a prominent feature in *Xunzi* in the third century BCE and in Wang Chong at the turn of the millennium. See *Xunzi* 21: 74ff. (Knoblock 1988–94 vol. iii 109) and Wang Chong *Lun Heng* 71, *juan* 24, 994ff. (Lloyd 2002: 32).

4

The Argument from Language

Human beings are not the only living creatures that can communicate with one another using sounds and gestures. In recent years our knowledge of the ways in which many other animals do so and how rich those communications can be has increased enormously. We even now know that plants too can communicate with one another: they use mainly chemical signals, though obviously their repertoire is limited (Tsing 2015, Daly and Shepard 2019, cf. Haraway 2008, Pollan 2013). Among animals, one much popularized example is that of meerkats who indicate to other meerkats not just to beware of a predator but also what type of predator is in the offing, jaguar, eagle, or snake (Manser, Bell and Fletcher 2001). Cheney and Seyfarth 1990 have shown the same for vervet monkeys. In some cases the meerkat and vervet signals can be picked up and interpreted not just by conspecifics but by other species of animals. Bird-song especially has been studied intensively, in work that reveals the very considerable variety of songs that some species (not all) are capable of (Catchpole and Slater 2008). Language in the broad sense of conveying some information, to conspecifics and to others, is certainly not just a human attribute.

Yet of course the degree of articulation of other creatures' modes of communication is far less than that of any human language.[1] This remains true even though a very recent article by Dediu and Levinson (2018) undertook a re-examination of the genetic, palaeontological and archaeological evidence to argue that the Neanderthals were fully

---

[1] The extent of the linguistic capabilities of the great apes continues to be a matter of controversy. Washoe was a chimpanzee who was taught certain elements of sign language (Premack 1976, Premack and Premack 1983, Gardner, Gardner, and van Cantfort 1987), but the issue is how much new understanding Washoe would be capable of without the benefit of human teachers, and the answer to that is precious little (Pinker 1994). Animal intelligence in general has of course been the subject of very considerable bodies of research (e.g. Griffin 1984, 1992), with Godfrey-Smith's study of the octopus (2016) a striking recent example.

Intelligence and Intelligibility: Cross-Cultural Studies of Human Cognitive Experience. G. E. R. Lloyd, Oxford University Press (2020). © G. E. R. Lloyd.
DOI: 10.1093/oso/9780198854593.001.0001

articulate beings whose linguistic capacities have generally been much underestimated. Yet so far as direct, not inferential, evidence goes, human languages alone show highly complex syntactic structures and semantic capabilities.

At the same time the very variety of human natural languages, as we call them, has two immediate consequences that are relevant to our inquiry. On the one hand, that variety increases the range of what we can hope to understand, for that is not limited to what those who speak our own particular mother tongue have to say. On the other, the fact that some of our interlocutors express themselves in a different language increases our difficulty in understanding them. To be sure we can never attain a *perfect* understanding of any speech act in any language. The problem of understanding is certainly not just a problem of translation but one of any communication. Not even what may appear to be the simplest of such acts has a fully determinate single meaning, not least because every context in which it is uttered is open-ended. As we remarked before, with most language use, we can and should distinguish word meaning from sentence meaning, and both of those from utterer's meaning (Grice 1968, 1975, 1978) and all of those from what interlocutors understand to be the message. For ordinary purposes we make do with more or less accurate conjectures of what is intended, bearing in mind that errors are liable to occur. Some of those we may hope our interlocutors will be able to correct, though some may be the result of their deliberately misleading us, as we shall be considering again in Chapter 6.

The range of natural languages spoken across the world is, as noted, huge, though the rate at which they have been dying out has been increasing (Crystal 2002, cf. Ladefoged 1992). Yet any such language will exhibit certain properties and it is one task of this chapter to explore some of these with a view to determining some of the key strengths and weaknesses of language as a tool of communication. If we are to study what we all, as humans, share, it is as well to begin with some of these commonalities.

The grammar and morphology of different languages vary, but every language is in possession of a vast array of general terms. Indeed the only exceptions will be proper names. Tiddles is a cat, but calling Tiddles a cat depends on a notion of where she belongs among animals. Going up the taxonomic hierarchy, that will relate her to many other animals that include lions and tigers in what we call the cat family. Going down that scale again, we distinguish between different kinds of domestic cat, Siamese, Persian, or whatever. All of that depends on what we apprehend as the similarities and differences between individuals, sub-groups and groups, whether or not we can give some explicit (whether superficial or deep) justification for the groupings we presuppose.

So the first utterly obvious point is that all languages depend on similarities and differences. The networks of general terms we use presuppose more or less well-ordered relations of likes and unlikes. As language-users all humans have in common that they apprehend such relations. But four fundamental points immediately complicate the picture. First the particular similarities and differences we recognize vary in part according to the language we are using at the time. Second, in our appreciation of similarities and differences we are not limited to those that a particular language conveniently picks out for us. So if the first factor operates as something of a constraint, the second suggests how it may be circumvented. Third, we must ask how far it is possible to lay down rules to distinguish the similarities and differences that are in some sense given by the data from those constructed by the observer—the problem of objectivity. Fourth, what different people assume about the character of the logical relationships we label 'similarity' and 'difference' may and does vary.

Let me offer a few elaborations of each of those points. As to the first, we are all familiar with the way in which certain languages make distinctions that are ignored in others. French recognizes the distinction between bone (os) and fish-bone (arête) which is masked in English insofar as we tend to use the single word 'bone' for both. Chinese use the term *yang* for both sheep and goats.

But that takes me straight away to my second point. Even though the Chinese use the same word for sheep and goats, they are perfectly capable of recognizing and describing the differences between them, indeed they have ways of indicating most of the differences between the fourteen or so closely related species of Caprines that they may encounter at the eastern end of the Eurasian land mass, as was shown by Wang Yiru in her study of the beginnings of sheep husbandry in Western China (Wang 2017).

The similarities and differences we recognize are certainly not limited to those our particular natural language discriminates for us. The point is perhaps most vividly exemplified by colour terminology, a subject which has, however, been much muddied by the search, from Berlin and Kay (1969) onwards, for basic colour terms and for a common sequence in which they are acquired. The main flaw in that cross-cultural pro-gramme was that many of the terms indigenous peoples were reported to have used when questioned about their perceptions were not primarily colour terms in the first place, but words to make other distinctions, for example, that between the fresh and the living on the one hand and the dry and the dead on the other (cf. Lloyd 2007: ch. 1, citing Conklin 1955 and Lyons 1995 in particular). But for my purposes here the lesson of other parts of the study of colour perception is clear. Human subjects are generally perfectly well able to draw distinctions between hues that go far beyond those that correspond to the vocabulary of their given natural language (Baylor 1995). The limitations of an existing vocabulary can be compensated for by introducing new names for hues, as is regularly done for marketing purposes in commercial contexts.

My third point is especially important. Are the similarities and differ-ences we recognize perceived or otherwise given by the data, or are they imagined or constructed? Are they discovered or invented? Take Rim-baud's suggestion that each French vowel corresponds to a colour, E is white, I red, U green, and so on. That would seem to be quite arbitrary. Experiences of what is called synaesthesia have been extensively researched and reported (Baron-Cohen and Harrison 1997) but the extent to which Rimbaud's intuitions are endorsed by other French speakers is controversial as is the question of how far they are mirrored in the vowel systems of other natural languages. Meanwhile I have noted just now the difficulty of settling on a 'basic' cross-cultural colour taxonomy.

A more obvious example of arbitrary associations would be the ancient Greek notion according to which a name or noun corresponds to a given number. The letters of the Greek alphabet were indeed used also as numerals, alpha for 1, beta for 2, gamma for 3, iota for ten, rho for a hundred, and so on. But that meant that the name Alexandros comes out as 521 (1+30+5+60+1+50+4+100+70+200). Not all Greeks were fans of such associations. In his *Metaphysics* 1093a13–28, Aristotle in particular is contemptuous of some of the ways the Pythagoreans played around with the symbolic associations of the number 7.

Of course many other similarities look to be far less arbitrary, indeed not in the least so. Those between members of what we call the same species of animal or plant can be justified on firmer grounds, their capacity to produce fertile offspring, their genetic make-up, their chromosome number. Yet even in that instance the questions of the objective reality of our favoured taxonomies and of the very notion of species itself continue to be vexed. Where in earlier taxonomic studies natural species were assumed to be fixed, indeed eternal, Darwin's evolutionary theory showed how mistaken that was. The relative orderliness of the higher species at the top of the scale breaks down in the apparent disorder among the lower eukaryotes and the prokaryotes, a matter partly of the paucity of data to go on in the fossil record, partly of the difficulty of interpreting it (Lloyd 2007: ch. 3).

Just about any and every claim that similarities are independent of the observers who apprehend them is open to challenge and claims for objectivity far harder to sustain than is commonly supposed (Daston and Galison 2007). However, that does not undermine the basic point I am interested in here, namely that it is indeed similarities and differences, however arrived at, whether by perception, inference, imagination, or invention, that are the relationships that we use in our efforts to understand and to communicate whatever it is we believe we have understood to others.

My fourth point relates to the variety in the accounts given or presupposed concerning the nature of similarities and of differences themselves. Some languages have, but others lack, an explicit vocabulary that draws a distinction between saying that one item is other than another and saying that it is different from it. Equally, there may or may not be clear ways to distinguish between saying that A is like B and saying that A is identical with B. Saying that A is different from B in certain respects does not rule out the possibility that it is similar in others, but a focus on difference may distract attention from coexistent similarity. In an earlier study of Greek philosophy (Lloyd 1966) I examined how, even in the most sophisticated and logically astute thinkers, a statement of difference may be thought to preclude similarity, when differences are treated as polar opposites deemed to be both mutually exclusive and exhaustive alternatives. In conversational exchanges the presentation of a pair of opposites as such forces a choice between them, masking the possibility that they may be compatible and that other options may be open.

Let me give just a single striking example to illustrate the point, from Plato, no less, who was one of the first Greeks to attempt to clarify the nature of contradiction when he insisted, in the *Republic* 436bff., for instance, that when opposites are asserted of a subject, it is essential to specify respect, relation and time when considering whether these are true contradictories.[2] Yet in the *Phaedo* 78dff., Socrates, having asserted that the Forms, of Being, Equality, and Beauty, for instance, are always constant and unchanging, then puts a question about particulars, the many beautiful things such as men or horses or clothes. 'Are they constant, or quite the opposite to those, never, so to speak, identical either with themselves or with one another in any respect?' This elides the third possibility, that those many beautiful things may be subject merely to occasional or eventual, not constant, change—a move that is used to gain agreement to a more extreme position than strict logic would legitimate, insofar as the contradictory to 'always the same' is 'not always the same', not 'never the same'.

Analogously possible confusions arise and are common in the understanding of relations of similarity. I devoted two extensive studies (Lloyd 1966 and 2015) to showing how widespread a reliance on analogy is in both relatively naive and highly sophisticated attempts to make sense of the world. On the one hand, the heuristic powers of analogy are obvious, not least from its use in Western physics and cosmology since the seventeenth century (Hesse 1963). On the other, the assumption that two items that share known characteristics will also exhibit similarities in others has often proved misleading. There is, to be sure, no algorithm to tell in advance where positive similarities give way to negative ones or differences. The history of speculative thought, and not just in the West, is one of a struggle to distinguish the two and sift the valid analogies from merely deceptive similarities.

---

[2] 'It is clear that the same thing will never submit to doing or suffering opposite things, in the same respect, at least, and in the same relation and at the same time' (*Republic* 436b, Lloyd 1966: 139). Socrates goes on to say that those conditions are not fulfilled in the case of a man who stands still but moves his hands or his head, or in that of a spinning top, which has a circular movement with respect to the circumference but is at rest with respect to its vertical axis, for it does not incline to one side or another.

Those points about the relations of similarity and difference in turn may be related to certain syntactic features of a given natural language. Much attention has been paid to such questions as whether a given language has a determinate term for the copula, whether identity statements are marked as such, how statements that imply the existence of certain items are distinguished from those that carry no such implication (Kahn 1973 for ancient Greek, Graham 1989 for Chinese). The scope for uncertainty, even confusion, on what 'similarity' and 'difference' themselves imply, within a given language, is great. That just increases when attempts are made to parse what is said in one language in another.

Sapir (1949) and Whorf (2012) went much further, though the thesis they promulgated comes in stronger and in weaker versions (cf. Leavitt 2011). In the strongest version language determines thought, in the weaker it merely exercises a fundamental influence on it. The more extreme view runs up against two obvious possible objections, first that some understanding of what is expressed in one language can be conveyed, however laboriously, in others, and second, that very different world-views are expressible within a single natural language. The most that should be conceded is that the syntax and semantics of a given language may serve to make certain distinctions more salient to its users than would otherwise be the case. The example I have discussed elsewhere (Lloyd 2018: 59–60) is the existence, in ancient Greek, of a battery of grammatical structures to express the different modalities of conditionals. Yet the suggestion that Bloom made (1981) following Sapir, that ancient Chinese is incapable of expressing counterfactual conditions, is given the lie not just by plenty of actual instances where they are entertained but also by the existence of a particular phrase, namely *jia shi*, literally 'falsely supposing', to pick them out. That is just one example, among many, where an apparent desire to prove some thesis about language determining thought has been backed up not just with weak, but with false, evidence and arguments.

If as the language-users we are, we are particularly dependent on our apprehension of similarities and differences, the fact that, as we said, the similarities and differences we focus on differ (whether given in our language or not) is one way of identifying one of the greatest obstacles to mutual intelligibility. Over a large range of mundane tasks of discrimination, there may be little room for misunderstanding. We understand that we are being asked to pass the salt and we pass the salt. That it is salt that is being requested is not usually open to doubt, even though what may be believed about salt, its symbolic significance or value, for instance, may vary, as too may customs concerning how to perform the act politely and with due deference to the customs of the group in question. To pick up a point from my discussion of felicity in Chapter 3, in the family in which I was brought up it was commonly held that if salt is spilt, a pinch of it should be taken in the right hand and thrown backwards over the left shoulder. That was one in the eye for the devil.

But when more highly charged beliefs and practices are involved, two interlocutors may have such different notions and values that mutual understanding is hard, or some may conclude impossible, to achieve. This may happen not just when members of very different cultures encounter one another, as when a missionary or an anthropologist encounters an indigenous society, but also within any given group however advanced or sophisticated it may pride itself on being. The priest lifts the chalice high above the altar, blesses its contents and then dispenses not wine, but the blood of Christ to the congregation. The devout accept the mystery of the Sacrament, though if they are questioned, the accounts they may offer of precisely what happens in transubstantiation may well differ. But the non-believer continues to see what is in the cup as wine.

One reaction to such a situation, as I have intimated, is to register that the beliefs of the believer and the non-believer are incommensurable with one another and to conclude from that that there is no way of arriving at any mutual understanding. Yet while in this particular religious context the two may indeed be pretty much at a loss, that certainly should not be taken to imply the impossibility of any meaningful communication between them. While strongly held beliefs about the Sacrament may separate them, when they share their more mundane activities (if indeed they are allowed to share them) they may find that they have far less difficulty in understanding one another. Outside the context of the Eucharist, wine is wine, and bread is bread, and the two interlocutors may share not just a meal but an understanding of what precisely that consists in. They may choose to differ on the Sacrament, but come to appreciate, at least to some extent, what belief or non-belief means for each other (cf. Chapter 9).

The hazards of communication are not to be underestimated, within a single language (with its multiple idiolects) even before we grapple with translations across different ones. When words are not used, but rather gestures or body language, these are even more liable to be misinterpreted. What to one observer may seem like cheerful giggles may to another be a sign of embarrassment or even shame. The influence of the contexts within which a communication takes place, and the roles and status of those involved, may be crucial. As we noted before (Chapter 2) what is appropriate when talking to children may be unacceptable among adults. One of the things we understand about fairy stories is that they are not intended as anything but fairy stories. But then just how seriously eulogies to those in authority are meant may be anything but transparent, as indeed are the calculated insults delivered by those, such as the fools in medieval European courts, whose role it is to do so (cf. Billington 2015).

But faced with these and other obstacles and impediments it would be ridiculous to lose sight of the reverse point, the success of much communication, statements, inferences, questions, commands, reprimands, praise, insinuations, jokes, however imperfectly those messages may be conveyed. It is undoubtedly of the greatest importance to be wary when statements or behaviour appear to be totally unexpected and not to conform to anything in our own ordinary experience. But while, as we said, earlier commentators often reached for the label 'irrational' in such circumstances, that was often premature, a confession of bafflement maybe, but one that should not be taken as a sign of the total impossibility of any understanding. The resources available to us to make at least some progress towards relieving that puzzlement are considerable and start—we said—with the mundane communications that proceed without encountering fundamental blockages.

We recognize after all that language is being used and that means that some array of similarities and differences is being brought into action. So the question is, as we said, which similarities and which differences are being deployed. How are those articulating tools being used by the speakers of the language in question? Even though we may temporally be at a loss, persistence should secure some progress starting with the common-or-garden and spreading out towards the more obscure. After all language is always used to communicate something, even when the message is that that thing is a mystery, a closely guarded secret, a truth that is implied to be beyond the reach of the very audience to whom the communication is addressed.

None of this is to ignore or to downplay the difficulties of understanding we face whenever issues of importance are discussed, not just between languages but within any given one. The work of interpretation requires determination and there is no guarantee of even modest success. Yet the very endeavour of attempting such interpretation implies that the interlocutors start from the assumption that intelligibility is possible, that some understanding is within reach, even though its imperfections and revisability must be acknowledged.

Two final issues should be faced. One might object, first, that the notion that some intelligibility is possible is indeed just an article of faith. Second, if one acknowledges, as one must, that there are occasions when understanding is beyond reach, how should the line of demarcation be drawn between the possible and the impossible?

To the first difficulty, one should ultimately reply that the possibility of intelligibility cannot be underwritten by some appeal to a more fundamental principle. The only proof or recommendation possible is an indirect one, the recognition that if such a possibility is denied, there is nothing further to be said and no communication is possible.

But that reply just makes it all the more important to have some positive guidance on the second difficulty. If our experience that we are able to understand others is fundamental, our recognition that understanding sometimes breaks down or an earlier interpretation must be revised reminds us of the need to acknowledge both limits and mistakes. But then the tactic that should be recommended at that point is not to diagnose an irremovable obstacle, but rather to investigate particular subject matters to review the particular conditions that each may present. I shall return to the general question of limits in Chapters 6 and 7, and will then devote four further chapters to examine particular areas of experience and knowledge, in an endeavour to analyse the conditions that apply in each. As we shall see in the final chapter, the conclusion to which we are drawn acknowledges the differences in the degree of difficulty in attaining understanding in different areas of human experience, while holding on to the basic point, that some understanding, however limited, however provisional, is within reach.

5

The Argument from Sociability

The second feature that links all humans together, alongside and connected with our use of language, is that we are all social animals. Here too, recent studies of other species of animals have brought to light how elaborate their social organization may be, where there is a trade-off between the interests of the individual and those of the group as a whole. Yet the possible range of varieties of interactions among humans is far greater than anything we can find elsewhere in the animal kingdom. Using our special skills in language, we engage with others in argument, inference, persuasion, to evaluate ends and work out the means to achieve them, including devising institutions that can promote our ability to undertake and implement such deliberations. Some of us are more talented than others in those social activities. The contexts in which we deploy those talents are very diverse and that may well affect the assessment of relative performance. But Aristotle's observation, that all humans participate in such activities, as the social animals we are,[1] holds true as a broad generalization.

Indeed that point has been revived and expanded by recent studies that have focused on the essentially social role of reasoning. Nicholas Humphrey in 1976 mounted an argument for the social role of intellect (cf. Dunbar 1998, 2009, Boyd, Richerson, and Henrich 2011). More recently Mercier and Sperber (2017) have argued that reason is not geared to be used in isolation. Rather, its primary role is to justify our beliefs and actions to others, and to convince them of their correctness, and conversely to evaluate the justifications and arguments they address to us. In any case humans cannot, in general, survive in total isolation.

---

[1] At *Rhetoric* 1354a3ff., Aristotle remarked that everyone shares to some extent in both rhetoric and dialectic, since all endeavour to uphold an argument, to defend themselves, and to accuse. Yet in *On the Heavens* 294b7ff., he notes as a weakness a particular tendency we all share, which is to conduct our inquiry not in relation to the subject-matter in question itself, but rather to our opponent in argument.

Intelligence and Intelligibility: Cross-Cultural Studies of Human Cognitive Experience. G. E. R. Lloyd, Oxford University Press (2020). © G. E. R. Lloyd.
DOI: 10.1093/oso/9780198854593.001.0001

Even hermits depend in certain respects on non-hermits, for they started life as children in some society or other.

Yet to see what, in respect of sociability, we all have in common on the one hand, and where we differ from one another on the other, is trickier than might at first appear (cf. Runciman 1998). Much depends on how we assess the impact of different modes of exchange, starting with linguistic interaction. We have mentioned before (Chapter 1, note 5; Chapter 2, p. 16) the evidence that shows that even in some predominantly oral societies there is an appreciation of the virtues and vices of argument. The Barotse, studied by Gluckman, we said, conceded that the Whites with whom they came into contact possessed superior technology, but they prided themselves on their own superior rhetorical skills. They were heavily involved in debates both on matters of policy and on legal cases. In neither context did they have written constitutions or codes of law to refer to, meaning that arguments invoking tradition and custom were always contestable in ways that could not be resolved by appeal to such evidence. Yet speakers and audiences alike were keen connoisseurs of the skills needed in persuasion and of the characteristics that a true statesman or a good judge should display.

On the other side, to be sure, there are other groups, and sections of our own society, indeed, where there is little or no self-consciousness about where arguments are sound and where they go wrong. I write this at a time when the category of 'fake news' calls for repeated comment in the media, even though there is little explicit analysis or even discussion of how precisely to detect its fakery. It is assumed we can, but a naïveté in that regard is sometimes exploited by the fakers themselves.

Given the immense diversity of social and political arrangements that are attested across the world, in modern and indeed also ancient societies, any attempted taxonomy is hazardous. Some are highly centralized polities, with authority concentrated in the hands of a tiny minority who justify their right to rule by appeal to birth or military prowess or wealth or, it may be, superior knowledge and experience. But others are more egalitarian and some have no equivalent to individuals (Head Men or Head Women) who take all the important decisions.[2] Of course why

---

[2] Fortes and Evans-Pritchard (1940) was an early attempt at surveying the variety of political systems in contemporary African societies.

more or less monarchical, oligarchic or democratic regimes have sprung up, and the reasons that they survive, or fail to, over extended periods, are questions that continue to baffle both historians and sociologists,[3] as well as politicians keen to immerse themselves in historical studies in the hope of learning lessons for their contemporary situation. Indeed the desire to use the past as a guide to the present or the future, according to the programme summed up in the dictum *Historia magistra vitae* (Koselleck 1985), constantly runs up against the barrier of the ultimately contingent nature of historical circumstance.

But the fact of great political diversity does not detract from the importance of the one generalization that continues to hold, namely that as the humans we are, we are all social animals. To be sure the extent to which we can exercise our potential in that respect does vary. When Aristotle spoke of 'political animals' he assessed the participation of different groups in the political process very differently. Women were not to be full citizens, nor were the considerable numbers of slaves. The children of citizens had no political function until they reached adulthood, and then only the males participated fully. Yet even while Aristotle largely endorsed the hierarchies that structured the city-states he was familiar with, it was not males whom he defined as political animals, not *andres*, but *anthrōpoi*, that is, humans. He certainly denied that many humans are capable of the highest form of philosophical reasoning that he considered the chief constituent of human happiness or flourishing. But all humans are capable of intelligence, deliberation, calculation, and persuasion: all have their contributions to make to social well-being even if those contributions differ in value. He was himself living proof that one did not have to be a full citizen in the city in which one lived in order to engage in philosophy, for, born at Stagira in northern Greece, he was after all himself not a citizen but a 'metic', that is a resident alien, at Athens.

It is true that other political regimes have treated large segments of the human population as less than human, denying that they belong to the human race or at least to some chosen sector of it. Yet even in the process of excluding groups from society, that endorses, in a perverse way, the connection between humanity and social belonging, while attempting to

---

[3] I shall return to this question below, p. 46, and in Chapter 7.

deny the biological facts of the first and equally operating an exclusiveness concerning what is to count as the second. While an acceptance of others' customs, roles, and values has often been in short supply, we can see that when any attempt is made to redraw the boundaries of humanity and of social participation that still recognizes a link between them.

Socialization starts, of course, with the society into which a person is born, and as with the natural language one first acquires, this may present a double bind. Learning one's mother tongue (as we call it) may be both a liberation and a constraint, a liberation because it gives one access to all the possibilities of communication that language offers, but a constraint in that one may too readily assume that the categories of that first language are the only valid ones. That is less likely to be the case if one has the good fortune to be born into a polyglot community. But even there the difficulties of seeing not just *that* the concepts inherent in a given language may need revision, but *how* to revise them may be considerable—as I am repeatedly stressing throughout these studies.

The analogy with language breaks down insofar as there is no exact equivalent, in political regimes, of living in such a polyglot community. True, we may have direct acquaintance with different types of social arrangements, in the family or the workplace, and the degree to which political regimes exercise a direct control over those varies. But some control is inevitable and that has an impact on the appreciation of possible alternatives. Given that social cohesion may be thought to depend on adherence to deep-seated customs and practices, calling them into question may be both intellectually difficult and politically and socially hazardous. In most societies there are considerable forces at work maintaining the existing social arrangements, minimizing the risks of dissidents challenging the status quo. This may be no mere matter of those in charge of education getting the young to believe what they should believe, and to behave correctly according to the norms of the group. To the effects of verbal persuasion may be added those of physical force. The sanctions available to those in authority to maintain their position range from the psychological to the use of whatever violence the laws or customs permit (Runciman 2009).

So if the answer to what all humans have in common in this domain is clear, namely the fact of living in communal groups, the ways in which those groups differ pose two main kinds of problems. Are the differences such that the universal rule of human sociability is under serious threat? Then how far do those differences undermine any claim we might make about the possibilities of mutual understanding across different groups of human beings? I shall use the extensive evidence from ancient societies, Greece and China, as usual, especially, to throw light on both issues, but first some general remarks are in order.

On the first issue much depends on whether the argument I used to confirm the universal rule can itself be upheld generally. I put it that even the attempt to exclude certain groups as human itself assumes that what marks out humanity is sociability. Those who might appear to be human fail the test, on this exclusive view, because their behaviour, their customs, and their social arrangements do not pass muster. Yet those who would exclude certain humans and deny their humanity are not so much denying the link between humanity and sociability as protesting that the range of what is properly human and properly social is far narrower than I have been assuming.

To counter that denial takes one, of course, to the second question, of how far mutual understanding can be achieved across individuals and groups that have very different conceptions of what it is to be human, or to be social. Stark divergences in beliefs and practices certainly exist. Persuading those who deny others' humanity that they are mistaken has generally proved difficult if not impossible. Aristotle at a similar point conceded that persuasion fails and maintained that one has to reinforce argument with threats of punishment and the law (*Nicomachean Ethics* 1179b4ff.). Yet while we have surely learnt, in the last century and this, that blind prejudice has ultimately to be resisted by force, that does not mean that on the conceptual point one should capitulate and concede that humanity and sociability are the prerogative of only a few of those who on other grounds we recognize as conspecifics. The arguments for an inclusive concept of what it is to be human must and can be defended even while we acknowledge that values and attitudes differ profoundly.

Let me turn to some concrete ancient contributions to the debate to get a grip on the range of possible views that have been taken on that vital question of what makes human beings human. Both ancient Greece and ancient China provide important evidence to help answer the three interlocking questions we have broached in this chapter, the diversity of human social groupings, self-conscious reflections on that, and the implications the answers have for the prospects of mutual understanding. Of course plenty of other ancient and modern societies also provide similar opportunities, but my aim here is to make the most of these two well-documented cases.

On the face of it the similarities between the situation in China before the unification achieved by Qin Shi Huang Di in 221 BCE and that which obtained in ancient Greece in the sixth to fourth centuries seem quite striking. Relatively small independent polities vied with one another engaging in frequent warfare. But in China the pattern of the political arrangements in their Warring States was more homogeneous than in the archaic and classical Greek city-states. Where in China the agreed ideal was that of the benevolent rule of a wise king, in Greece monarchic or tyrannical regimes were interspersed with oligarchic and democratic ones, even though we must concede that full democracy, such as that established in Athens by Cleisthenes in the sixth century, took some time to develop.

Of course Chinese rulers were surrounded by their ministers and advisers, and the importance of choosing wise and independent ones is repeatedly stressed in different types of writings that otherwise express very diverse views on ethics and values. But the ultimate decisions, and not just on political matters, rested with the king, and later, after the unification, with the emperor. There was no counterpart to the Greek practice of determining which policy should prevail by assessing what the majority supported. In Greece that might be by acclaim or by secret ballot, and those who participated varied from a restricted group of citizens to the entire citizen body, although that never included women or slaves. In China disputes between rival advisers are well documented in the histories, from the *Shiji* onwards, and a wide array of both historical and fictional ones is a leitmotif in the *Zhanguoce*, the *Intrigues of the Warring States*, a compilation put together in the first century BCE.

It would be very difficult to claim that the quality of the decisions taken depended on how far they had been debated openly and settled by majority vote. The record of the best-documented Greek democracy, Athens, shows that the Assembly could be as arbitrary and as short-sighted in their decisions as any autocrat, as indeed several ancient commentators protested. The opportunity to get a policy overturned was there and was not infrequently taken, as in the famous Mytilenean debate,[4] and it is obvious that frequent such changes had just as destabilizing an effect as those of a single ruler who prevaricated. But it can be urged that in the open situation of the Greek Assemblies and Law-Courts (Dicasteria) no one individual or group had a more privileged position in the decision-taking process than any other. The Assembly opened with the question 'Who wishes to speak?' Although some individuals were expected to be more likely to wish to do so than others, in principle anyone could stand up to address his fellow citizens.

Now the circumstances in which some Greek city-states adopted democratic regimes rather than oligarchic and monarchical ones have been and continue to be the subject of great controversy.[5] Preference used to be given to an argument that the development of hoplite warfare led to a call for greater enfranchisement beyond the old ruling elites (Snodgrass 1965). Others have argued that other factors, such as the development of overseas trade or the monetary economy, contributed to those elites losing their exclusive grip on power (Seaford 2004). But one has to concede that no single hypothesis or set of them provides anything like a conclusive explanation. For our purposes here, we may simply note that we have here good evidence for political diversity but remark also the continuing similarities in the fundamental human practices of arguing, persuading, inferring. The numbers of individuals participating in political decision-taking increased with the advent of democracy, and so too did those who made a career as advisers in the matter of success in public speaking. But while the pragmatics of the exchanges in the Assemblies were very different from those of Chinese courts, the basic human endeavours of engaging with others in argument remained essentially similar.

[4] When the citizens of Mytilene revolted against Athenian hegemony, the Athenians repressed that with force. An Assembly back at Athens decreed that all the male citizens should be executed and the women and children enslaved and a ship set off for Mytilene with orders to that effect. But the following day the Athenians repented. Those who had objected to that decision called a second Assembly at which it was revoked, and a second ship was dispatched to reach the island before the orders carried by the first could be carried out. Thucydides 3. 36ff.

[5] Ostwald (1969) and Finley (1973/1985 and 1983) were influential early contributors to the debate, which continues in the writings of Dunn 1992, 2006, 2018, R. Osborne 2007, 2010, and Cartledge 2009, 2016 especially.

But we have yet to consider how Greek and Chinese thinkers them-selves reacted to their experiences and recorded their sense of the similarities or differences between different human polities. What can they tell us about the answers to our two other questions, to do with what differentiates human groups and how far mutual understanding is pos-sible? Both those ancient societies were acutely aware of the differences between their own populations and other human groups with which they were familiar. Both have a sense that those others are 'barbarians', falling short in one or other aspect of the civilized behaviour they themselves held and manifested as the ideal. Yet, as we noted before, both included those others in the category of human being, *anthrōpoi*, *ren* (人). In the third century BCE text put together by Lü Buwei, the *Lüshi chunqiu*, 19.6.2, we are told that while what separates different human groups are such items as languages, customs, dress, taste, what unites them all is feelings, especially the need to satisfy certain basic desires. Even back-ward tribes, such as the Man and Yi, are 'one with us and the same as us in satisfying their desires.' On the Greek side too, while Aristotle is well aware that very few humans live in city-states, *poleis*, he is absolutely clear that humans qua humans are political (*politika*) animals.

Yet when it comes to identifying what marks out humans from other animals, there is a difference between what we find in the third-century BCE Chinese writer, Xunzi, on the one hand, and Aristotle on the other. While Aristotle pinpoints reason, *nous*, as the differentiating factor, in *Xunzi* (9. 162, Knoblock (1988–94) vol. ii 103–4) it is a sense of right and wrong, *yi*. So, while for Aristotle the criterion relates to psychology (in his sense, that is to cognitive faculties), for Xunzi it is a matter of morality. Yet that may tend to exaggerate the contrast. Looking more closely at Aristotle's views of the cognitive faculties, we should bear in mind first that he does not deny intelligence (*phronēsis*) to animals, only theoretical reasoning and the deliberation that reflects moral judgement.[6] So certainly he would have no quarrel with Xunzi's idea that morality is confined to humans.

---

[6] Following the classic study by Detienne and Vernant 1978, I analysed what Aristotle owes to common earlier Greek perceptions of the *mētis* (cunning intelligence) of animals such as the fox, the spider, the bee, and the octopus in Lloyd 2013.

Neither thinker would have endorsed the position of those who nowadays attribute some inklings of a moral sense, or at least of reciprocal altruism, to certain species of animals (see de Waal 1991, 1996 and 1998 on chimpanzees and Seyfarth and Cheney 1984 on vervet monkeys). Both, however, were very much aware of the problem of how human children develop the moral sense that is essential to their role in society. Aristotle denies that the young have moral choice. He is faced with the problem of saying how and when this happens, though if challenged on that subject, he would no doubt have fallen back on the bare assertion that it does. Meanwhile Xunzi, for his part, devotes much of his attention to the analogous problem he faces. Against the view of his predecessor Mencius, he puts it that humans are naturally not good, but evil (*Xunzi* 23: *xing e*). But that means that they need all the help they can get to achieve the desired goal; that is, of becoming 'gentlemen' (*junzi*). Accordingly, educating the young is as important a preoccupation for him as it was for Plato or Aristotle.

Both the Greeks and the Chinese were acutely aware of the strangeness of the languages and the customs of the peoples by whom they were surrounded. The Greek term *barbaros* suggested that those peoples just made repetitive noises, which they caricatured as 'bar-bar'. But that did not imply that their languages were incapable of conveying information and ideas. The Greeks may have been rather bad at learning others' tongues, even Latin when they came under the domination of Rome. But they were familiar enough with the members of other societies learning to speak Greek. Foreign slaves, after all, had to, to obey their Greek masters' orders. When Socrates uses Meno's slave, in Plato's dialogue, to conduct a little experiment he hopes will show that knowledge is recollection, he first checks with Meno that the slave speaks Greek (*Meno* 82b)—which he does, since he was born into Meno's household, though many other slaves did not have Greek as their first language. Yet for the Greeks, as for the Han Chinese, the basic humanity of *anthrōpoi* and of *ren* (人) was not cancelled by the fact that other humans spoke in such a different way, had such different customs and did not share the same ideas about the good order and good government of society.

So what does this brief survey suggest on our major questions of the uniformity and diversity of humans and our mutual intelligibility? The appreciation of diversity does not undermine the commonalities of what it is to be human, which revolve, among other things, around the two main factors we have identified; first, having language—some language—and second, belonging to a social group—in some kind of society. True, there have been those—there still are—who deny the humanity of the members of other groups, on the periphery of their own polity or even within it. We noted that these humanity-deniers are often beyond persuasion. They adopt values that are irreconcilable with our own, though to identify the members of those they deem to be subhuman, they can be confronted with what we would see as the need to make a concession however reluctant they would be to agree. Insofar as those other peoples have languages and form societies, they share in the defining characteristics of humans even with those who would deny their humanity.

However, the more we argue for at least a limited commonality and mutual intelligibility across human populations, the more we need to address the question of why understanding fails in the first place. This is the topic of my next chapter.

6

Turning the Tables

Obstacles to Mutual Intelligibility

Given that we are all language-users, and further that we are all naturally social creatures, living and interacting with our fellows, the questions we are interested in might be turned around. We might ask *not* how and why we manage to understand one another, but rather how and why we ever fail to do so. Of course one reason why we may not succeed is that our interlocutors are hell-bent on deceiving us or at least are not doing their best to help us to understand. But what about occasions when that is not the source of the problem and we may presuppose sincere attempts at communication between senders and receivers?

Obviously the diversity of languages, and the differences in social and political arrangements, customs, and values, are often an impediment, but not, I have argued, an insurmountable one. Even when we disagree with what others say or how they behave, that disagreement generally presupposes some understanding. We may encounter languages whose syntax and semantics seem quite alien to us. Yet that does not usually prevent us from making some progress towards comprehending them. It is true that some writing systems have yet to be decoded. But when they are, there is no reason to expect the messages they convey to be radically different from those carried by those languages we can understand. The as yet undeciphered Linear A script may well turn out to be used for purposes that are familiar enough from other writings, if not Linear B, then some other one. Of course it may not: but as the writing system it was, its main function, most would say, would be to deliver intelligible messages to someone.

Where living languages are concerned, we can and do find interpreters who can help us, and with perseverance we can even begin to acquire some competence in the language in question ourselves. I hear perhaps

Intelligence and Intelligibility: Cross-Cultural Studies of Human Cognitive Experience. G. E. R. Lloyd, Oxford University Press (2020). © G. E. R. Lloyd.
DOI: 10.1093/oso/9780198854593.001.0001

as many as twenty different languages being spoken in the streets and College bars of the highly cosmopolitan city of Cambridge. I consider myself fluent in three apart from English. I can carry on a reasonable conversation in two more, I am up to polite exchanges in several more and I have varying degrees of familiarity with a number of ancient languages where there are no living speakers to help and correct me.

But the problem arises, as we said before, not so much in mundane transactions, as when we encounter seemingly quite baffling statements, expressions of strange beliefs, weird inexplicable behaviour. The difficulties become exacerbated when a group insists that it has a monopoly of the right way of doing things and of the correct understanding of the world around us. They may even go so far as to adopt the extreme position I mentioned before, of denying that those who have different opinions and customs are proper human beings at all. I shall need to return to that view. But our first task is to review some typical kinds of situation in which our efforts to achieve a modest level of understanding meet considerable obstacles.

One such is when our interlocutor reports an intensely personal, private experience. As James showed in his classic *Varieties of Religious Experience* (1902), it is in the nature of mystical experiences that they cannot be shared or communicated to others. The outsider appreciates that the mystic has undergone some heightened, exceptional experience, but the words and even the gestures and images used to convey some idea of its content are all avowedly inadequate to the task. This is not so much a case of misunderstanding as one of not having any basis on which to arrive at any secure detailed understanding whatsoever. It is not so much that communication is incomplete: rather, the only thing that is communicated is that an intensely private experience has occurred. The trouble is that when words fail, they fail. We are then sometimes left with what have been called 'empty concepts' which may have a particular potency but that are not supposed to be understood as conveying content in the way ordinary terms do (cf. Chapter 9).

More commonly obstacles to mutual comprehension may be thought to arise at the level of the basic assumptions that are being made about reality, the world and the subject's place in it. Philosophers are in business to answer such existential questions, often in direct competition with other philosophers. But as has recently become a topic of much debate within social anthropology (e.g. Holbraad and Pedersen 2017, Laidlaw 2017),[1] whole groups of people may share certain implicit presuppositions that go to make up a distinct ontology and these ontologies may be radically different from one another. When such opposing ontological schemata come into confrontation, the difficulty of achieving any mutual understanding may be thought to be extreme. Indeed it is at this point that recognition that there is no neutral vocabulary in which to describe such schemata may tempt one to the conclusion that such understanding is impossible, for on that view these are worlds between which no communication is possible.

Yet as I have argued before, that counsel of despair can and should be resisted. We can and should concede, to be sure, that no understanding is ever perfect, within the confines of a single ontology, let alone across several. But the inference to total mutual unintelligibility arises from a single-minded focus on deep-seated ontological assumptions to the exclusion of contexts and occasions when mundane transactions are carried on with at least a degree of success. The anthropologist or the missionary may be acutely aware that the group they are in contact with makes quite different assumptions from their own about animals, plants, the dead, the ancestors, and individual persons and what it is to be a person, let alone on issues involving values. The studies of Marilyn Strathern in particular (e.g. 1988) have revealed how in many societies persons are not so much individuals as 'dividuals', defined as nexuses of relations, where the relationships are what count not the items so related. The latter exist courtesy of the former, rather than being assumed to be independent substances.

But none of those considerations stops the anthropologist or the missionary from sharing in the everyday activities of the group and communicating with its members on many such matters. The participants in the conversation may have very different views about why it rains but still agree on the fact that it has begun to rain. They may react very differently to someone being bitten by a snake, and give quite different explanations of that event, while still sharing the knowledge that that is what happened. The criteria for adequacy in communication

---

[1] Notable earlier contributions to this debate which goes back to Viveiros de Castro 1998, include Henare, Holbraad, and Wastell 2007, Turner 2009, Pedersen 2012, Descola 2013, Taylor 2013, Laidlaw and Heywood 2013, Holbraad, Pedersen, and Viveiros de Castro 2014 and Viveiros de Castro 2015.

thus vary with the context and with the content of the message that is being communicated.

The differences in the ideas and practices that have been associated with distinct ontological schemata run deep and the possibilities of misunderstanding are far-reaching. It may take profound immersion in another culture, its knowledge systems and practices, its ideas about where it stands in relation to other cultures, and to the other living beings by whom they are surrounded, to begin to avoid such mistakes. But that is not to say that no progress can be made. To reiterate the fundamental point, the fact that no comprehension is perfect should not lead us to underestimate the extent of the successful interpretations that anthropologists often achieve, not just on those mundane matters I have spoken of, but even of the profoundest commitments of the peoples they study. After all, it was only after such an immersion in the whole life and experiences of indigenous cultures that anthropologists felt confident enough to describe the underlying ontologies and to point out where they differed from their own. Those accounts indeed describe often startlingly different systems of thought and practice, but not ones that are impossible to explore and to report on to the very different audience the anthropologists address in their studies.

While the ontologies the anthropologists discuss have much in common with the metaphysical systems of philosophers—they all in some sense offer accounts of reality or what there is—they differ in their levels of explicitness and in the scope and reach of their significance. The ontological schemata in anthropology are generally inferred rather than direct reports of statements spontaneously made by indigenous informants. This potentially has important implications for how they should be understood, since outsiders are often at a loss to reconstruct the range of the original commitment and the pragmatics of the actual communicative exchanges on which the anthropological accounts are based. Nor do those who record such exchanges always pay sufficient attention to those matters.

Thus as regards the first point, Hugh-Jones (2019) has recently argued that in reconstructing views on the relations between 'humans' and other 'animals', for instance, it is essential to ask how far it is indeed 'animals' in general that are in question—which raises the issue of whether there is indeed an indigenous category that corresponds to 'animal', just as we have also queried whether our interlocutors have concepts that are exactly equivalent to our 'person' or to 'agency' or to 'nature'.

Second, as we have said before, whether a story is told on solemn ritual occasions or is just an account to keep the children quiet can make a considerable difference. That is a very obvious point. But plenty of excellent anthropological monographs are eloquent testimony to the deep and long-drawn-out processes of adjustment their authors underwent as they gradually came to achieve some greater understanding of the peoples they were studying.[2]

Yet one interpretative device that used to be quite common carries its own hazards and is one that I have criticized before (Chapter 1). This was when some strange or apparently counter-intuitive statements were claimed to be intended not literally but merely figuratively. The first problem about such a move is that the contrast between literal and non-literal, for example, metaphorical, meanings was often not an actors' category but an imposed observers' one. In that case, strictly speaking the option of claiming that the paradoxical statement was not intended to be taken *au pied de la lettre* was not open to the native informant. Yet that leaves as a puzzle the question of the *force* of the statement, where indeed we may now no longer be in a position to recover the pragmatics of the exchange, between native informants and anthropologist observers. That registers the ongoing difficulty of interpretation and does nothing to resolve it. But it may serve to underline the importance of the general hermeneutic need for background information particularly on the contexts of the exchange (cf. Sperber 1985, 1997, Mercier and Sperber 2017).

We have more to go on where we are dealing with what is indeed explicit philosophizing. At least this is the case when the philosophers offer clear propositional statements of their positions and back them up with arguments, including those that aim to justify the basis on which their claims are made. Yet here the problem is the cost that that clarity has to pay in terms of applicability to real life situations.[3] Obviously

---

[2] Among exemplary instances of such monographs I may mention Christine Hugh-Jones (1979), Stephen Hugh-Jones (1979) and Descola (1996) especially.

[3] The fifth-century BCE Greek philosopher Parmenides argued with evident conviction that change is impossible and insisted that that is a conclusion that reason shows, even though he admits that it conflicts with what perception suggests. Yet as the living human being he was, he was undergoing change at the very moment when he was making such claims.

when we encounter two strictly contradictory assertions, we cannot assent to both. If one and only one of such a pair can and must be true, the second must be dismissed as false. That does not make it unintelligible, to be sure, but the challenge would be to say how anyone could entertain it. However, the actual practice of philosophical discussion is often anything but totally transparent. Transparency is secured where the participants face a choice between what are dubbed wffs (well-formed formulae) whose interpretation is not open to doubt, but wffs are in practice rarer in actual philosophical debate, let alone in ordinary conversation, than many would like to assume. In other instances we would be dealing not with a strict contradiction but a merely apparent one.

So the illusion that a choice has to be made should often be resisted. The history of philosophical speculation—and not just in the West—offers scores of examples where fundamental issues in cosmology, ontology, ethics, and psychology have been opened up in often anything but constructive dispute. Even if I do not sign up to the idea that metaphysical problems just stem from confusions in language, we can detect plenty of instances where a certain opacity has muddied the debate, even though, paradoxically, this has often led to the fruitful exploration of original ideas.

Take the controversies that date back to antiquity on the questions, first, of whether the cosmos is eternal or created; second, of whether all physical events are causally determined; and third, whether the chief good for humans (the *summum bonum*) is pleasure or virtue. The first thing we may notice is that the alternatives presented are sometimes not pairs of contradictories (true alternatives) but contraries. The contradictory of the assertion that the cosmos is eternal is the statement that it is not eternal. The contradictory of the statement that the *summum bonum* is pleasure is the statement that it is not pleasure. That means that it is possible to deny both that it is pleasure and that it is virtue without contradiction, leaving open all sorts of possibilities of what it may be, and that may include the reaction that the question as posed is misjudged.

But aside from these elementary logical considerations, the chief difficulty often consists in the obscurity of what any of those statements is committed to. What does the 'cosmos' include? How are we to understand the assertion that any object is 'eternal'? The modern-day cosmologist would insist that to talk of either the eternity or the creation of the universe implies some framework incorporating a notion of space-time and some understanding of how before and after are to be judged. Those were certainly not in the forefront of the minds of those ancient thinkers who debated the issues with such passion. In my second example one might ask both what counts as a 'physical event' and what notion of 'cause' is in play, where ancient as well as modern texts testify to a variety of ideas about that. In my third example obvious questions arise concerning how 'pleasure' is construed and whether a 'highest' good excludes other goods or goals that are somehow 'below' it.

Not only is there systematic obscurity in the positions that are being discussed, but the contexts in which the debate is held are sometimes left out of account in interpreting its contents. We may feel that we cannot doubt Socrates' seriousness, as he is portrayed by Plato, but that same Plato leaves us in no doubt that many of those he called sophists were not interested in philosophical inquiry. They were out to show how clever they were at bamboozling their audiences, when indeed they were not actively cheating and deceiving them, even though they often simultaneously hoped that their brilliance in argument would lead some of their listeners to sign up to the further instruction they offered. In India too, as we can tell from the accounts of debates in the *Upaniṣads*, some were held merely to entertain the court. In others victory at all costs was the goal and as we saw before, the defeated party could face public humiliation.

The conclusion we should draw is not, of course, that the opacity of some philosophical debate rules out any possibility of understanding nor that the clarity it achieves with well-formed formulae always comes at the cost of a realization that they represent an idealized not a practical situation. But it underlines the hard work that has to go into interpretation, not just when that means digging deep to identify the underlying implicit assumptions in play, but also in contexts where we are offered what purport to be clear and explicit statements of carefully thought-out points of view. Language, we said, enables effective human communication over every aspect of life and thought. But for successful communication to take place, sender, message, and receiver have all to cooperate in a context where there may be no alternative channel by which success or failure can be judged. While the pragmatic consequences of the receipt of a signal are often good enough indication of a modest success,[4] we have emphasized before that perfect mutual understanding is never within reach and we should settle for the realization that a provisional grasp is all we can hope for. Yet recognizing it may be provisional means also recognizing that it may, with imagination and hard work, be modified, revised, and improved.

But does an insistence on the possibility of some limited understanding not run into the difficulty that has so often dogged Western attempts to comprehend the beliefs and values of other societies, ancient and modern, namely that those attempts presuppose that those Western interpreters occupy some privileged position, an Olympian vantage-point from which everyone else can be assessed? Does this not savour of Western assumptions of cognitive superiority over all others? Anthropologists, philosophers, and historians in Western societies may all have distinct motives for engaging in the effort to understand others, but that inquisitiveness is surely widely shared. It is more and more the case that anthropologists report on the curiosity that indigenous peoples exhibit about the foreigners with whom they come into contact. In a way these peoples come to practise anthropology themselves on the anthropologists and missionaries who have come to investigate them. This is a particular feature of the work of Viveiros de Castro (e.g. 1992) and Vilaça (2010) especially.[5]

Contact with 'modernity' quite often elicits a considerable effort to study and comprehend, and many polyglot groups exhibit greater linguistic skills than most of the members of modern industrialized societies. To be sure, such efforts require as a prior condition a desire or will to understand, where we come back to the questions first of sincerity and second, of the influence of values and assumptions about humanity. But while that qualifies, it does not totally negate, the claims for the possibility of limited mutual intelligibility that I have been making.

---

[4] To pick up my earlier example, using whatever natural language we choose, my friend hears my request to pass the salt, and duly passes it to me.

[5] Kopenawa and Albert (2010/2013) contains what is, to date, perhaps the most sustained piece of indigenous anthropologizing.

Yet how that claim works out in practice, in several of the key areas of human cognitive endeavour, has yet to be examined in detail. After a discussion of evolutionary issues in the next chapter, I shall devote four more to investigating that claim where 'mathematics', 'religion', 'law', and 'aesthetics' are concerned, where in each case the important basic methodological principle we should adopt is not to prejudge what each of those labels presupposes.

So let me now hazard some concluding remarks concerning the nature of the obstacles to mutual understanding that we may encounter. First, there may be question marks over the intentions and motives of one or more of the participants in the exchange. Some may be more concerned to conceal than to reveal their true beliefs, where secretiveness and obfuscation shade into positive mystification, even deceit. Second, there is the inherent opacity, or certainly open-endedness, of many speech acts in ordinary conversation but especially where profound beliefs or values are at stake, whatever the natural language used and in whatever context. We all delight in using our imaginations to convey deep thoughts and feelings, but that very imaginativeness may baffle our interlocutors.[6] Third, we must always factor in the information available as to the pragmatics of the communicative exchange and that is often in short supply. Then fourth, where understanding behaviour is concerned, we are often faced with the graver problem of arriving at some idea of what certain acts signify either to those who perform them or to their possible audiences. The answer in terms of tradition, the statement that that is the way we have always done it, may be true, but tends just to push the question one stage further back, to the puzzles of how the tradition itself came to be established, how it is maintained and what originally it was taken to mean.

As we have remarked, consideration of the obstacles to understanding has sometimes led to the conclusion that in certain circumstances it is impossible. But our examination of why communication does not always succeed serves as a reminder that it sometimes does. Armed with an

---

[6] That is not just a feature of some convoluted exchanges in sophisticated highly conventionalized situations, such as philosophical debate, for it may occur whenever speakers are intent on doing justice to the importance of what they glimpse as new insights. On that story our cleverness and originality may be one of the main obstacles to our intelligibility. But what human is going to settle for expressing just what has already been expressed before?

awareness of what can go wrong, we can be more confident that we can make some progress in understanding our fellow human beings even while we respect that their views differ from our own.

There are, to be sure, many problems that lie beyond the reach of even the latest developments in science, in physics and cosmology, in biology, in psychology, sociology, and of course history and anthropology themselves. In some instances it may be that no solution will ever be attainable and certainly the experience of the progress of science is that our appreciation of what we still do not understand grows with the growth of what we do. But faced with the problems of understanding not the world, but one another, counsels of radical despair, I suggested, are premature and can be resisted. For we all, after all, have the resources of language and the common experience of sociality on which to base our efforts at some, limited, mutual understanding, even while that may well be at the price of modifying and revising our own initial assumptions. The challenge of radical otherness, as I have put it before, may then be seen not so much as a threat, rather as an opportunity, though we shall point out in later chapters how very demanding that may be.

7

The Evolutionary Issues

The issue between the two contrasting points of view I have been considering, the first advocating the basic uniformity of human cognitive, conative, and affective faculties, the second stressing their diversity, comes to the fore in the sharpest possible way when attempts are made at developmental, that is, evolutionary, arguments. Once Darwin had shown how species have evolved, by descent with modification, one particular traditional religious view, that humans were unique among animals in having been created in God's image, became increasingly difficult, not to say impossible, to maintain. While *The Origin of Species* (Darwin 1859) had relatively little to say about humans, no one could fail to notice the applicability to us of the arguments it advanced about other animals, as of course Darwin himself was later to spell out in *The Descent of Man* (1871). Indeed ever since, what in most people's view evolutionary studies have succeeded in encompassing has been growing steadily, to include not just anatomical and physiological phenomena but also behavioural and psychological ones.

Obviously for survival humans needed both a certain combativeness and a certain capacity for cooperation. Both many of the kinds of intelligence humans show, and some of the characteristic flaws in our reasoning, are shared to some extent by other animals. As I have mentioned before, to survive in the jungle or on the savannah any creature will need what has been called, in humans, fast and frugal reasoning, though it is only humans who can reflect self-consciously on that. A capacity to cooperate with conspecifics also carries a clear evolutionary advantage (cf. e.g. Runciman, Maynard Smith, and Dunbar 1996, Dunbar 2009). In order to ensure that a certain mode of altruism is not exploited by individuals who just pursue their own interests, other species besides us have evolved cheater detection mechanisms, designed to bring deviants back into line (Dunbar 1999). Yet again it is only

Intelligence and Intelligibility: Cross-Cultural Studies of Human Cognitive Experience. G. E. R. Lloyd, Oxford University Press (2020). © G. E. R. Lloyd.
DOI: 10.1093/oso/9780198854593.001.0001

humans who have developed a moral vocabulary to distinguish right from wrong.

Such observations do not take us very far, but to get to grips with the underlying questions I may use a recent study by a leading neuro-scientist, Antonio Damasio (*The Strange Order of Things*, 2018). Dama-sio takes up the challenge of offering a Grand Synoptic Theory to account for the broad sweep of evolution from the simplest unicellular organisms to human cultures. The focus here is especially on homeosta-sis, the principle of self-regulation that is at work in the simplest cell all the way up to the feelings that Damasio identifies as the main motivating forces at work in what we call culture. He asks (2018: 26–7) 'is it conceivable that feelings could have motivated the intellectual inventions that gave humans (1) the arts, (2) philosophical inquiry, (3) religious beliefs, (4) moral rules, (5) justice, (6) political governance systems and economic institutions, (7) technology and (8) science?' And he answers his own question with a resounding 'yes, wholeheartedly'.

But two problems, both relating to the diversity of the phenomena those eight categories cover, immediately arise. The first is whether it makes sense to attempt cross-cultural generalizations about each of them, about what, for example, 'the arts' comprises in different cultures (the topic of Chapter 11), and similarly with 'philosophical inquiry' 'religious beliefs' (Chapter 9) and even, maybe, 'science'. But then even if we put that difficulty about cross-cultural categories to one side for the moment, there is still the major problem of how the evidently diverse manifestations of these various activities can be accounted for by appeal to factors that are common to all human beings. Damasio's argument is that the origin of human and indeed animal feelings can be traced back to much earlier sources in evolution. But that leaves little room for a diversity in feelings themselves, and some diversity must evidently be factored in at some point, if we are to explain the differences in the end results. Otherwise why do not all human cultures enjoy precisely the same artistic experiences, practise the same mode of philosophical inquiry and the rest?

Where Damasio's argument was anticipated by ancient writers, both Chinese and Greek, and where it was not, are alike instructive. I mentioned before (Chapter 5, p. 47) the passage in the third-century BCE text, *Lüshi Chunqiu* that agrees with Damasio insofar as it puts it that what all humans, Han and non-Han, have in common, are certain feelings, while it recognizes great cultural differences between different peoples. Even more striking is the comparison with Aristotle. He identified the search for pleasure and the avoidance of pain as the main basic factors governing behaviour, in both humans and other animals. Other creatures do not engage in abstract reasoning. But they have perception and, more importantly, appetite and so pursue what is pleasant and avoid the painful, many deploying their practical intelligence (*phronēsis*), even their cunning (*mētis*) to do so.

Thus far he can be said to be close enough to Damasio's basic focus on feelings. But aside from the fact that Aristotle had no evolutionary theory, he diverged from Damasio in insisting that we humans can and must be trained to feel pleasure and pain correctly, that is in accordance with what is truly pleasant and truly painful respectively. Those are topics in which it is easy to be mistaken, for appearances may deceive, not just in the matter of what is pleasant, but also what is painful. His invocation of choice, *prohairesis*, not only drives a wedge between what is true of children and what applies only to adults, but also allows for cultural divergences. Although all humans are by definition 'political animals', the character of the political associations they form has a major impact on their values and behaviour, on what they consider to be pleasant and painful, indeed.

The differences between those ancient and modern theorists serve to identify a dilemma. For any view that focuses solely on the natural biological processes of evolution the difficulty is to account for the diversity of human cultural experience. Differences between different animal species can be explained in terms of the search for and occupation of specific biological niches. But as the biological species we are, humans all share essentially the same, at least a common, niche. Here basic human uniformity runs up against the evident diversity of human cultural products. But conversely, if we focus just on that diversity, the differences in artistic appreciation, religious experience and the rest, that runs the risk of ignoring or downplaying what we all have in common as the social animals we all are.

Evidently, neither type of monocausal hypothesis can account for the complexity of the data we are endeavouring to explain. Neither a theory that takes natural evolution as the sole source, nor one that focuses exclusively on 'culture', will do. More importantly, if we run through the eight items that Damasio identified (as noted above, p. 61), there is no reason to think that precisely the same mix of factors is at work in all of them.

Let me give just three further examples over and above those that will be discussed in subsequent chapters. Let me concentrate here on philosophical inquiry, technology and science. The character of the philosophical investigations undertaken by different individuals and groups within different societies differs profoundly and not all cultivate a taste for such investigations even on the broadest construal of what counts as 'philosophical'. Some concern for questions to do with morality is universal, though how that concern expresses itself is very varied. Some groups do, others do not, engage in explicit discussion of the bases of knowledge (epistemology) for instance, while the self-conscious analysis of argument schemata (logic) is rare in ancient and not even very common in contemporary societies. We may agree that successful philosophical inquiry yields its own intellectual pleasure, but it cannot be said to assuage basic human needs, such as those that have to be satisfied where the necessity for food, for shelter and for reproduction is concerned.

Again we may agree that pretty well every human group has a mastery of certain techniques notably in relation to hunting, cooking, and agriculture. But the complexity of the technology developed in that and other contexts varies enormously. Nor do all the instruments and tools in question serve to secure our basic subsistence. Some of the most intricate devices invented by ancient societies were geared to entertainment and display. Pulleys serve multiple purposes in building construction, but they were also put to use, in ancient Greece, to create Hero's elaborate automatic theatre, designed purely to amaze and amuse an audience (Berryman 2009: 139–43). As we shall be considering again later (Chapter 11) the feelings invoked by the playing of musical instruments varied and vary from an intense pleasure at the beauty and appropriateness of the sounds to disgust at the immorality they were thought to promote. It has accordingly proved extremely difficult to identify cross-cultural universals in the responses to musical phenomena: in just about every case we have also to take into account the specific reactions that reflect the values and associations of particular cultures.

My third example is science, where of course the question of whether science is a peculiarly modern and indeed Western phenomenon, dating from the so-called scientific revolution, continues to be hotly disputed (Kuhn 1970, Cohen 1994, 2015, Crombie 1994, Huff 2011, cf. Lloyd and Vilaça 2019). I have argued elsewhere that science should not be defined in terms of its end results (for they are always open to revision) but rather in terms of its methods and ambitions, the observation, classification, prediction, explanation, and understanding of physical phenomena. Those aims are widespread and while the explicit invocation of something like an experimental method is rare, the use of trial and error procedures is common enough. Yet that does not make 'science' a single universal and uniform human attainment. Rather, that term covers an amalgam of attainments that have very different manifestations in different contexts. The historian's task is to ascertain the specific nature of the scientific ambitions, successes and failures, of any given group at any given historical juncture, where 'scientific' picks out the endeavour to understand and control the environment and depends on the skills of observation, classification, and trial and error procedures that I have mentioned.

To repeat, where all eight of the items in Damasio's list are concerned, a balance has to be struck between the universal and the culturally specific factors that appear to be responsible. It is as well to be reminded of what all human individuals and groups owe to our deep evolutionary past, not just what we share with our own human ancestors, but what those ancestors of ours had in common with close relatives from whom they branched off, the ancestors of other creatures living today. At the same time it would be foolish to ignore the very diversity in the cultural trajectories of different human groups since the emergence of *homo sapiens*. As I pointed out in Chapter 5, that all humans are social animals is ungainsayable, but the ways in which we organize our social lives are very different.

If we then ask the next question of why that should be so, we can make some limited progress by taking into account ecological factors, even geographical ones, though these have sometimes been rejected out of hand (cf. Acemoglu and Robinson 2012). The Eurasian land mass allows land communication between widely scattered populations and this has been argued to be advantageous insofar as exposure to very different types of diseases helped to secure a certain level of immunity to them (Diamond 1997). There is certainly good concrete evidence that the lack of immunity to typical European diseases wreaked havoc when the Spaniards arrived in the New World.

Yet first the ecological argument also has to face important counter-evidence. Amazonia, Africa, and Asia all provide examples where quite diverse political and social arrangements developed in groups that nevertheless enjoyed essentially similar ecological and environmental conditions. The distinction between highly hierarchical and broadly egalitarian polities cannot be correlated straightforwardly with particular such conditions (Hugh-Jones 1994).

Moreover, second, more ambitious theses concerning the political consequences of the agricultural revolution or of advances in technology are also difficult to sustain. It has been argued, to be sure, that at a particular level of development a certain critical spirit emerged challenging traditional beliefs and leading to new breakthroughs in culture and intellectual life. The commonest form such speculations take is varieties of what in the wake of Karl Jaspers has been called the Axial Age, comprising changes that were deemed to have swept across Eurasia from some time in the seventh century BCE to the fourth, though some would include developments down into the Common Era. Versions of this have been discussed not just by Jaspers himself (1953) but by Eisenstadt (1982, 1986), Bellah (2005), Baumard et al. (2015), and Boyer and Baumard (2018). Yet all such proposals face difficulties, not just in the chronology but also in the world-views of the leading figures who are held to be responsible. Zoroaster, Confucius, the Buddha, Socrates, and Jesus not only lived at different times—so the Axial Age, so-called, has to be stretched out over several centuries. But more importantly the mode of critical analysis they practised and the nature of their positive teaching, insofar as we can reconstruct that, varied, as also did the social and political conditions within which they worked and against which they were reacting (cf. Runciman 2009: 203, Lloyd 2014: 118–19).

The history of reflexive thought in very early times, like that of later periods indeed, is full of contingency. Why prominent individuals produced the ideas and theories they did is almost always going to elude any hard-edged explanation. Socrates evidently responded to the political circumstances of the society in which he lived, which certainly allowed and even cultivated open discussion—at least within limits—limits which his fellow citizens held he had transgressed. But Socrates' views on morality, justice, education, cannot be said to have been determined by those circumstances. No more can we exactly give any explanation for why Plato took it upon himself to produce a series of literary master-pieces that built up a particular representation of Socrates, and we have only to refer to Xenophon or to Aristophanes to see that there was nothing inevitable about Plato's interpretation of his teaching.

The promise of evolutionary theory does not in practice get to be fulfilled beyond a very limited point. It gives us a tolerably firm grasp of the evolution of much of the great variety of animals for which we have living or fossil records, although there are plenty of questions still to resolve. These include the precise effects and indeed the causes of the Cambrian explosion and of the various extinction events for which we have evidence. But while we can anchor the emergence of humans in a story about hominids and other higher primates, the diversification that then characterizes the further development between different groups within the one human species repeatedly eludes our best efforts to comprehend.

We might have expected that where basic spatial cognition is concerned, there would be easily identifiable human universals. It has been supposed, for instance, that everyone must make use of a basic contrast between right and left. Yet as Levinson and his colleagues especially have shown, that is refuted by the ethnographic and by experimental evidence (Levinson 2003, cf. Lloyd 2007: ch. 2). There are human groups that adopt an absolute framework of spatial coordinates, determined by the cardinal points, north, east, south, and west, rather than either the intrinsic or the relative systems of spatial organization that we are more generally used to (see Fig. 7.1).[1]

---

[1] The 'intrinsic' system involves an object-centred coordinate system, where the coordinates are determined by the 'inherent' features, siddedness or facets of the object used as ground. Thus in English we may speak of the 'front' of the TV or car, that being the side we attend to, and another object can be located 'in front of the TV' in relation to that side. But in some languages the inherent features are directly based on shape, where human or animal body parts provide prototypes (e.g. when we speak of the 'foot' of the table). The second, relative, frame of reference presupposes a viewpoint given by the location of a perceiver and a figure and ground distinct from that, as when we say that one object is 'to the left' of another, namely from a particular viewing position. The third, absolute, frame of reference is determined by the cardinal points, north, east, south, and west.

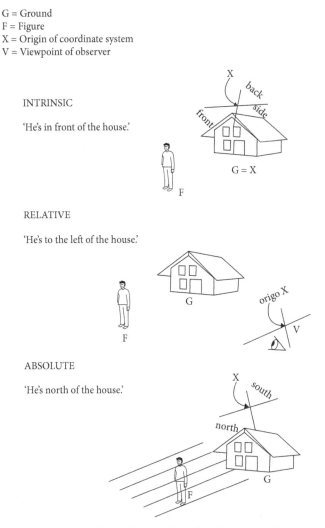

G = Ground
F = Figure
X = Origin of coordinate system
V = Viewpoint of observer

INTRINSIC

'He's in front of the house.'

RELATIVE

'He's to the left of the house.'

ABSOLUTE

'He's north of the house.'

Fig. 7.1 Systems of spatial coordinates. Based on Levinson 2003: 40.

Moreover the groups in question, in Australia, in Siberia, in Meso-America, and in Africa, certainly do not share the same physical environment, so once again that cannot be held responsible for the differences.

Here, then, we have clear evidence of a certain divergence in the cognitive capacities of different groups of humans or at least of their preferential uses, though we can recognize all of them as modalities of *spatial* cognition. Translation between them may be problematic, but as Levinson shows, certainly not impossible. Besides in some cases one modality may be combined with another. In English we can and do deploy all three in different contexts. The skills required in using each differ and carry corresponding advantages and disadvantages in navigational abilities. The use of an absolute frame goes with an extraordinary skill in tracking movement, yet this is achieved, in Levinson's view, at a high price, namely a serious cost in terms of the focus of cognitive attention. The coordinate system must be constantly updated as the individual moves through space.[2]

Some still put their faith in the idea that what falls to the side of nature will eventually be clearly delineated from what belongs to culture. But that dichotomy proves harder and harder to apply. In the first instance the difficulty stems from the revival of epigenetic arguments and the greater appreciation of the plasticity of genes (Keller 2000, Jablonka and Lamb 2014). The lesson, also, of my investigations here is not just to underline that difficulty, but fundamentally to call into question the validity of the nature versus culture, nature versus nurture binaries as adequate frameworks within which to discuss the problems.[3] Nature is often used to refer to what objectively exists: but first we have to recognize that the concept of nature is not universal across all human populations. I have argued elsewhere that it was a concept invented (not discovered) in a particular historical context in ancient Greece, and while the nature-theorists, the *phusikoi* or *phusiologoi*, were convinced that there are objective regularities in what they called 'natural' phenomena, there was much less clarity on what the realm of its antonym *nomos*, comprised, for that could be a matter of law, or of custom or convention.

More importantly, second, it is obvious that human beings are exceptional in the length of time it takes for our young to become self-sufficient—as even the Greek philosopher Anaximander is said to

---

[2] The navigational skills of both humans and other species of animals continue to elicit a massive research effort, though plenty of puzzles remain. See for example Lewis 1994, Hutchins 1995, and most recently Salmond (2021) on those of long-distance Polynesian navigators.

[3] Fundamental critiques of the nature/culture dichotomy have been mounted, in different contexts, by Strathern 1980 and Wagner 2016 especially, and cf. Kuper 1999.

have insisted upon in the sixth century BCE. That means that from birth onwards and throughout our early development we are exposed to a huge variety of broadly 'cultural' influences. It is true that from Piaget (1929, 1930, 1959) onwards (cf. e.g. Carey 1985, Carey and Spelke 1994, Carey 2009) developmental psychologists have argued that all human infants and very young children make the same or very similar assumptions in the areas that have been called 'naive physics', 'naive psychology' and 'naive biology'. But aside from the fact that most of the empirical investigations have to date been carried out on Western children (cf. Henrich, Heine, and Norenzayan 2010) the views that young adults come to entertain on those questions certainly soon come to diverge, as both ethnography and ancient and not so ancient history show. The notion of cleanly separating out what belongs to 'nature', our genes, and what to 'nurture', the way we are brought up and acculturated, becomes quite chimerical.

That does not mean that we should forthwith desist from speaking of the domain of nature as such at all, but it does serve as a reminder that that domain cannot be treated as a given, and whether any such concept has traction among the current human populations we study is problematic in the extreme. Conversely while we may assume that what falls to the side of culture is relative to a particular group, we should not lose sight of the point that I argued in Chapter 5, namely that the fact that humans live in societies and accordingly have some 'culture' is universal, even while the particular customs and values they adopt are not. On that score most human groups are aware of others who differ from themselves. But how those others are to be treated, and the relationships between those other humans and other living creatures, are further questions that have been answered very differently in different societies separated in time or space or both. Those are issues to which I shall return in my final chapter. But first we should pursue the questions of similarities and diversities in some specific fields of human experience, and first in one that deserves particular scrutiny since it is one where expectations of uniformity may be especially strong, namely in what we label mathematics.

Meanwhile the avowedly cautious conclusion I would draw from this inquiry is that, for all the advances made in studies of both biological and cultural evolution, we are still some way short of being able to provide a robust account of the commonalities and the divergences in human cognitive capacities that pose the initial problem for our investigation. On the other hand our discussion does supply us with good defensive arguments to resist grand generalizations, which is a point we shall need to keep in mind as we turn now to some more detailed inquiries.

8

Test Case 1

Mathematics

As members of modern societies surrounded by mathematical gadgets from calculators to computers, we may tend to assume that there is nothing particularly problematic about what mathematics is and what counts as mathematical. In shopping malls and markets across the world, two plus two equals four. Units of measure vary but the quantitative relations they are applied to exhibit their quantitative character everywhere.

Yet it does not take much reflection to identify some fundamental problems. What should our answer be to the questions of what exactly mathematics studies and of what precisely it covers? What is the status of the objects in question if indeed they are objects, or relations if they are relations? What knowledge, what truths, does mathematics yield and are the answers to those questions the same across the different areas we recognize as belonging in some sense to mathematics? It was all very well for Galileo to have proclaimed that the book of nature is written in the language of mathematics, but is there such a book—a script to be deciphered—and why should it have been mathematical?

Ethnography and history serve notice that we should not be overconfident that we know what mathematics is and what it does.[1] Even ethology also does. What mathematical skills do we attribute to bees when they construct their hexagonal cells or communicate foraging patterns to their conspecifics, and what spatial cognition should we ascribe to the many species of animals, from birds to fish to butterflies, that migrate over long distances?[2] Aristotle commented that spiders

---

[1] This chapter owes much to an intensive and protracted series of exchanges I have been privileged to enjoy with two colleagues, Professors Willard McCarty and Aparecida Vilaça: cf. also Lloyd and Vilaça 2019.

[2] Animals' sense of numerosity has been studied, e.g. by Dehaene 2011.

Intelligence and Intelligibility: Cross-Cultural Studies of Human Cognitive Experience. G. E. R. Lloyd, Oxford University Press (2020). © G. E. R. Lloyd.
DOI: 10.1093/oso/9780198854593.001.0001

(that is one species of them) estimate the centre of their circular webs pretty accurately (*Historia Animalium* 623a10). Ethnography in turn provides rich evidence of the variety of mathematical interests in different modern-day indigenous societies (e.g. Crump 1990, Ascher 1991, Urton 1997, D'Ambrosio 2006), though it has to be said that the data has been subject to much overinterpretation, especially with regards to the supposed ignorance or incompetence of the people in question.[3] That judgement sometimes results precisely from a failure to consider the different interests and values that may be in play. Not to engage in geometrical explorations in the style of Euclid does not imply incompetence in the manipulation of shapes. The lack of complex systems of enumeration may indicate not an indifference to all aspects of quantities but rather a different set of interests.

Vilaça's study of the Wari', who live in Rondonia province in Brazilian Amazonia, is exemplary for the care with which she explores not just their indigenous ideas and practices but also how they react to the missionaries and teachers who nowadays instruct them in the mathematics they think the Wari' need to live in modern society (Vilaça 2019 and 2021). For the Wari' the first two numbers have potent associations. The word for 'one' signifies the isolated, or the lonely, and it has a distinct negative connotation. 'Two', the first dyad or couple, by contrast, is positive. The terms they use for larger quantities vary according to context: thus to translate the Portuguese term for 'three', they use a word that properly signifies 'few', while for four they use their term for 'many'. Of course they recognize, as anyone would, that a haul of three peccari is 'many' when the hunter has just his own family to care for, but is 'few' if there is a whole village to feed. But only a very naïve outsider would suppose that they confuse a haul of three peccari with a haul of four. Where 'geometry' is concerned, Wari' women weave baskets that incorporate what we would describe as complex geometrical designs. But they say they do not do this courtesy of any verbal instruction. Rather, they learn the gestures by seeing them made by their instructors. What secures the transference of what we can call mathematical skills is the movement of hands, not verbal description.

---

[3] This is true in particular in relation to the mathematical competence of Pirahã speakers, where the basic data relating to their performance and interests is sharply contested (Gordon 2004, Everett 2005, Levinson 2005).

Thus the Wari' response to what the missionaries teach them is guarded. It is not that the Wari' are incapable of learning to count in the way we do, for they are taught this in schools, even though for large numbers they generally borrow terms from Portuguese—and indeed they have a remarkable talent for comprehending other peoples' perspectives. It is rather that in their ordinary lives numbering is not their concern, which is rather primarily with proper social relations and values. For our part, if we are to understand their uses of mathematical ideas and practices, we have to grasp their views on a whole range of other issues, on persons and what it is to be human, on the differences between different human beings and between humans and other animals, on the basis of sociality, on the human condition in short. Vilaça's challenging overall thesis is that the qualitative indefinition of the Wari' universe has implications for the quantitative instability of the sets that could be counted.

Similar lessons about different ways of doing mathematics, and differences in attitudes to different areas of mathematical activity, can be got from the considerable evidence we have of ancient ideas and practices from Egypt, Babylonia, India, China, and the Greco-Roman world, where I shall concentrate, as usual, on the particularly rich sources for the last two especially, for in both mathematics serves as a prime example of intelligent reasoning.[4] We can identify no fewer than five different topics on which divergent views were expressed. (1) What does mathematics study? Are there distinct mathematical objects and if so how do these relate to the phenomena of experience? (2) Do different branches of mathematics have indeed different objects? How do the objects of 'arithmetic' (numbers) relate to those of 'geometry' (shapes), not to mention those of such 'applied' studies as 'harmonics', 'astronomy', 'statics', 'dynamics', 'mechanics' and 'cartography'?[5] (3) What mode of cognition, knowledge or understanding does mathematics secure? (4) How is expertise in mathematics to be acquired? (5) What understanding

---

[4] On Egyptian mathematics, see, for example, Imhausen 2009, on Babylonian see Robson 1999, 2009 and Høyrup 2002. Robson and Stedall 2009 provides a useful survey of many other mathematical traditions as well. In what follows I draw on the materials I have prepared for a contribution to Fried's forthcoming volume.

[5] The dangers of applying these categories of ours uncritically should be stressed. This applies in particular to 'mechanics': see Berryman 2009.

of natural phenomena and the cosmos as a whole, including of the place of humans in it, is mathematics thought to yield?

Ancient Chinese mathematics has often been represented as purely practical in orientation. But that is to neglect not just their theoretical interests but also the considerable explicit commentaries in ancient Chinese texts on the issues I have just identified. Our two most important sources are the *Zhoubi suanjing*, dating from around the turn of the millennium, and Liu Hui's third-century CE commentary on the other early mathematical classic, the *Jiuzhang suanshu*. These texts provide precious evidence on what their authors thought about the last three questions on my list especially.

Thus in the *Zhoubi* there is a dialogue between the master Chenzi and his pupil Rong Fang, where the latter first sketches out what he has heard mathematics (that is calculation, *suan*, or *shu*, the art of numbers and figures) can deliver.

> Long ago, Rong Fang asked Chenzi 'Master, I have recently heard something about your Way. Is it really true that your Way is able to comprehend the height and size of the sun, the [area] illuminated by its radiance, the amount of its daily motion, the figures [or numbers *shu*] for its greatest and least distances, the extent of human vision, the limits of the four poles, the lodges into which the stars are ordered and the length and breadth of heaven and earth?'[6]

To which Chenzi answers that that is correct, though when Rong Fang attempts to investigate the problems, he fails several times before Chenzi relents and comes to his rescue.

But if that describes the scope of the subject (Q 3), the way knowledge is to be acquired (my Q 4) is distinctive. Chenzi puts Rong Fang's failure down to his lack of serious application. All these matters can be solved by mathematics [*suan*, calculation], and he can do it 'if he sincerely gives reiterated thought to them'. In Greece, in the Euclidean tradition at least, the pupil or reader is led inexorably from one step to the next, until the goal is reached, *quod erat demonstrandum*, QED—what was there to be demonstrated has been. Yet neither teacher nor pupil figures as such in

---

[6] I base my translations of *Zhoubi suanjing* 23–4 on Cullen 1996.

Euclid's *Elements* which is written in an entirely impersonal style. In the Chinese text, when Chenzi eventually explains the problems to Rong Fang, he attributes his earlier failure to his lack of application and his inability to cultivate his patrimony, rather than to a lack of intellectual grasp of an impersonal method that will deliver certainty. Besides, the criterion of success is not demonstration, but the ability to spot analogies and to extend categories. As he puts it, it is 'the ability to distinguish categories in order to unite categories' that is the key to success (*Zhoubi* 25.5). 'If one asks about one category and applies [this knowledge] to a myriad affairs, one is said to know the Way' (24.12ff.).

Writing a little later, in the third century CE, Liu Hui complains that mathematics, for which he too uses both terms, *suan* and *shu*, has come to be neglected by his contemporaries.[7] In a bid to restore its prestige he offers an account of the early development of the field, stressing its venerability and its cosmic importance. It originated, he claims, in the discovery of the eight trigrams (on which the chief Chinese divinatory system, set out in the *Book of Changes*, was based), in the inauguration of the calendar and the tuning of the pitch pipes. As in the *Zhoubi*, it is intimately linked to the *Dao*, the Way, manifesting itself in the primary interaction of *yin* and *yang*. Liu Hui tells us that it was those interests that led him to the study of mathematics and its various branches.

The text on which he is commenting, the *Jiuzhang suanshu*, deals with a wide range of topics, some arithmetical (as we would say) others geometrical, such as the study of the properties of right-angled triangles. But Liu Hui stresses the unity of the whole subject. The different branches (*zhi*), he says, all have the same root (*ben*). They have a single source or principle, *duan*. But that is not a matter of all stemming from a single set of axioms. Rather, the unity is a matter of the same procedures being at work throughout. Over and over again, as in the *Zhoubi*, the aim is to show the connections between the different parts of *suan shu*, extending procedures across different categories. The subject grows not by deduction, but rather by extrapolation and the discovery of new applications of basic procedures. The algorithms on which they depend can and should be checked: they are 'proved' in that sense

---

[7] Liu Hui's commentary is edited in Chemla and Guo 2004.

(cf. Chemla 2012). But there is no sense of any need to give axiomatic–deductive demonstrations of the results. Once Chinese mathematicians were assured their conclusions are sound, they did not worry about how they could be given any such demonstration, but turned, rather, to the next problem.

The texts we have considered give the lie to the view that the ancient Chinese never engaged on second-order reflection of the nature of mathematical inquiry. But Greek discussions of the issues raised by my five questions are far more explicit and bear witness to ongoing controversies stretching over several centuries. It is worth examining in some detail this evidence, from within a single culture, of plural approaches to what is nevertheless recognized to be the same general subject-area. On the one hand, the Greeks are the sources for many ideas that later proved to be influential in European mathematics. On the other, they certainly show that the answers to my five questions are far from foregone conclusions.

Thus on my first two questions, the objects of mathematics and the relations between its various parts, we already have good pre-Platonic evidence of divergent Greek views. The relationship between 'arithmetic', the study of numbers, and 'geometry', the study of shapes, was problematic from the outset. This is in part because 'number', rather *arithmos*, was usually defined in terms of a plurality greater than one, which in turn meant that one itself is not a number. The first number is two and fractions were generally understood as ratios between numbers. The notion that numbers form a continuum was accordingly not available. Geometry, on the other hand, was recognized to deal with an infinitely divisible continuum.

This differentiation meant that certain relationships that could not be satisfactorily expressed in terms of numbers could nevertheless be handled geometrically. The ratio between the side and the diagonal of the square, most famously, is incommensurable. Where we talk of the irrationality of the square root of 2, the Greeks spoke of the incommensurability of side and diagonal. But of course a geometrical construction of the square and its diagonal is perfectly possible and although the side and diagonal themselves have no common measure, those lengths are commensurable in square.

However, this left the major problem of reconciling the status of these two apparently very different objects (Q 2). In the fifth and fourth centuries BCE, two mathematicians, both associated with the Pythagorean school, took diametrically opposite views on that topic.[8] Philolaus is reported as holding that geometry is the 'source and mother-city (*mētropolis*) of the rest of the mathematical sciences' (Plutarch, *Quaest. Conv.* 718e, Huffman 1993: 193ff.). But shortly after him Archytas maintained the superiority of *logistikē*, that is the art of calculation (Fr. 4 from Stobaeus, Huffman 2005: 225). The fundamental problem was how to reconcile these conflicting views which surfaced again in a dispute in harmonic theory. There some writers treated sound as an infinitely divisible continuum while others insisted that concords must be expressible as ratios between integers (Barker 1989).

Yet the nature of the difficulty that stemmed from a realization of the incommensurability of the side and the diagonal should not be exaggerated. The old idea (Hasse and Scholz 1928) that it provoked a *Grundlagenkrisis*—a foundation crisis—in Greek mathematics simply does not tally with what we know of the very considerable developments that were made, not just by Pythagoreans but also by others, throughout the fifth and fourth centuries BCE. The first sustained piece of deductive geometrical reasoning is the work of someone who should not be represented as a Pythagorean, namely Hippocrates of Chios. His studies on the quadrature of lunes showed how certain curvilinear areas can be shown to be equal to other rectilinear ones (the problem often formulated in terms of that of squaring the circle). Hippocrates is also credited with the first attempt to systematize most of geometrical knowledge in a work of synthesis that later writers, probably overoptimistically, thought of as a precursor of Euclid's *Elements*. Archytas himself may have privileged arithmetic, but he produced a highly sophisticated discussion of the problem of duplicating the cube. This involved a complex geometrical construction determining a point as the intersection of three surfaces of revolution, a right cone, a cylinder and a tore (Eutocius, *Commentary on Archimedes On the Sphere and Cylinder* II, citing Eudemus, Huffman 2005: 342ff.).

On the basis of what we know of fifth-century mathematical studies it would be more plausible to argue that the discovery of the

---

[8] The evidence for Philolaus and for Archytas is collected by Huffman 1993 and 2005 respectively.

incommensurability of the diagonal and the side of the square acted as a stimulus to research rather than as a factor that inhibited it. That result came to be the subject of rigorous proof, one example of which we find in Euclid himself which proceeds by reductio ad absurdum (*Elements* Book 10, app. 27). If the diagonal and side are indeed commensurable, then it was shown that the same number is both odd and even.[9] That would be a self-contradiction: so the diagonal and side must be incommensurable. That was only one of many demonstrations of this result. However, the important point for us is that all such proofs exhibited the power of mathematics rather than its weakness and that certainly contributed to its considerable prestige.

By the time we get to the mid-fourth century BCE the controversies swirling round the issues raised in my five questions become even more tense and bitter, with ramifications far beyond what we normally rate as mathematics. The rich materials from Plato and Aristotle especially throw important light on what they thought about the relations between mathematics and cosmology and between mathematics and other areas of learning.

Plato was himself no practising mathematician. Yet he made heavy use of mathematics in his metaphysics, his epistemology and his cosmology. He was, to be sure, not the first Greek philosopher to insist on a contrast between, on the one hand, reason and its findings, and, on the other, sense-perception and its objects. Parmenides, especially, before him had opposed the Way of Truth, based on *logos*, and the Way of Seeming, on which mortals wander deluded by their senses and by their conventional beliefs. But for Plato this contrast came to form the basis for a far more systematic ontology. True, he nowhere sets out, in so many words, what we call his Theory of Forms, which is sometimes misnamed a Theory of Ideas, though it is clear that the Forms are *not* ideas or concepts, but the true realities. But in many different contexts the speakers in such dialogues as the *Symposium*, *Phaedo*, and *Republic* contrast Beauty,

---

[9] To paraphrase the proof: if the diagonal of a square (a) is commensurable with its side (b), let the ratio between them (a:b) be expressed in the lowest terms. But by Pythagoras' theorem, $a^2 = 2b^2$. So a^2 and also a are even. In which case b is *odd*. But as a is even, take a as $= 2c$. That means that $4c^2 = 2b^2$ and so $2c^2 = b^2$, which in turn means that b is *even*. But b cannot be both *odd* and *even*, so the original assumption that the diagonal is commensurable with the side must be rejected.

Goodness, Equality, and so on themselves, with examples of beautiful, good, or equal things. The latter suffer from a fundamental flaw. What is beautiful in some respect or at some time may be ugly in another or at another. Beauty itself, by contrast, is unqualifiedly beautiful. This does not lead him to suggest that perceptible particulars are unreal. They exist, but the way they can be said to be is qualified: they are 'never constant' as we saw in Chapter 1. The Forms alone are the true unqualified realities.

Mathematical examples figure prominently in his development of this contrast. A pair of equal sticks may be equal in some respects, but will inevitably be unequal in others. To discover what Equality itself is, we must direct our attention away from perceptible particulars and concentrate on the Form itself. Yet while mathematical entities are aids in developing our appreciation of the Forms themselves, they do not qualify as among the highest realities themselves, at least according to arguments presented in the *Republic*. There mathematics is praised as a training in abstract thought, but in the famous image of the Divided Line is subject to two shortcomings. On the one hand geometry uses perceptible diagrams: on the other, mathematics gives no account of its fundamental hypotheses, here represented by such examples as odd and even and various figures and kinds of angles (*Republic* 510c).

Eventually, though this is not clear in the *Republic*, Plato was said to have developed a notion of what came to be called mathematical intermediates. They share with the Forms the property that they are intelligible, but share with perceptible phenomena that they are plural (where the Forms are said to be unique, *monoeidēs*: there is only one intelligible object that is Beauty itself). So while mathematics has an important contribution to make in training us to practise abstraction, it is still rated below the highest mode of cognition, dialectic itself.[10] But quite how Plato wishes to sustain the claims he makes on its behalf is far from clear.

Mathematics, we learnt, fails to give an account of its starting assumptions. But how does dialectic do so? What kind of account is available to it that is beyond the reach of mathematics? We are told that the summit

---

[10] The Greek term *dialektikē* is cognate with *dialegesthai*, where the basic meaning is to converse. In the *Republic* and elsewhere Plato uses it as the name for the highest mode of cognition. But Aristotle demotes what he calls 'dialectic' and returns closer to the original usage.

of intellectual progress is a so-called unhypothesized first beginning, the Form of the Good. But how that is to be reached is left in abeyance. By the time we get to Euclid, indeed already by the time of Aristotle, the status of the axiomatic assumptions on which mathematics in particular was to be based was clarified. The primary propositions must be self-evident and indemonstrable, for if they are capable of being proved, they should be, and then they would not be primary. But obviously that insight into the nature of postulates cannot be applied to Plato's claims, for if we think of his 'hypotheses' as axioms, he would appear to be committed to the paradox that dialectic is to be based on an unaxiomatic axiom. Evidently the insights that can lead the philosopher to an appreciation of the Form of the Good must draw on other sources of inspiration than mathematics, a further reason for treating that as lower in the scale of cognitive capacities than his version of pure dialectic.

This is not the only puzzle in the programme of the *Republic*. When Socrates discusses the study of harmonics and astronomy he insists, in both cases, on the mistakes that arise from too great a focus on empirical evidence. At 530d he expresses his agreement with unnamed Pythagoreans that harmonics and astronomy are in some sense 'kindred disciplines' (a view found in Archytas Fr. 1, Huffman 2005: 103ff.), but he goes on to criticize one way of pursuing the former subject. This consists in attempting to learn about harmonies by studying audible sounds, indeed investigating these experimentally on a string, trying to determine which is the smallest audible interval, for example. What they should do is rather to consider which *numbers* are concordant with which others (531c). Similarly, certain astronomers are taken to task for attempting to make progress in their subject by studying the visible heavens. No, he protests (530bc), it is by means of problems that the true potential of astronomy to train us in abstract thought will be realized, and we should 'leave the things in the heavens alone'.

We have here, then, a programme of a radically anti-empirical practice of the mathematical sciences. That was certainly not the position of those Greeks who actually engaged in either harmonics or astronomy, but it serves as a prime example of the deployment of a certain interpretation of mathematics for philosophical or metaphysical ends. Philosophy, we are left in no doubt, is supreme. Mathematics can help us to learn to cultivate our reason. But in Plato's view in the *Republic* the price that has to be paid to achieve that end is to turn away from any attempt to strengthen the empirical basis for the mathematical sciences. His programme, in other words, was not geared to furthering those studies so much as to seeing what they can contribute to the education of the potential rulers of his ideal state, namely to help train them in abstract thought.

However, that is still not the full story where Plato is concerned. When he came to write a cosmological dialogue, the *Timaeus*, we can detect a certain accommodation to mathematics that goes beyond what we might have expected from the *Republic*. The *Timaeus* offers only a 'likely account' of the cosmos, while it still insists (29bc) that where the Forms are concerned, certainty must and can be attained. The chief respect in which Plato's cosmology goes beyond all its predecessors relates to the development of the idea that creation reflects the work of a divine benevolent Craftsman or Demiurge (Sedley 2007). But how does he go about his work, of introducing order into preexisting, chaotically moving, matter? Both the construction of the World-Soul and that of the body of the cosmos draw heavily on mathematical models. The world-soul is an elaborate arrangement of musical harmonies. And when it comes to what the cosmos is made of, the fundamental elements are represented by combinations of primary triangles, the right-angled isosceles, and the half equilateral. The four simple bodies, of fire, air, water, and earth, which Plato takes over from Empedocles and others, are not, in his view, true elements at all. Each is identified with one of the five regular solids, constituted by those primary triangles. Fire is identified with the tetrahedron, air with the octahedron, water with the icosahedron, and earth with the cube. The fifth regular solid, the dodecahedron, is mentioned but not identified with a simple body at *Timaeus* 55c.

Thus as a physical theory we are offered a variation of atomism. But where the original atomists, Leucippus and Democritus, had postulated an indefinite variety of atomic shapes, Plato's version shares the property of being geometrical, but diverges from theirs in insisting on strict regularity. The orderliness of the cosmos was, for him, a fundamental tenet and that feature was secured by the basically mathematical character of the intelligence at work in its creation.

Plato's cosmology, even when presented as no more than a 'likely account', is breathtakingly speculative and at points appears quite arbitrary. Yet his moral injunction to cultivate the soul, notably by the practice of abstract reasoning, and the epistemological basis of his whole philosophy, the contrast between the intelligible and the perceptible worlds, remained immensely influential in the West even while many dissented from other aspects of his teaching. First, those who actually pursued investigations in such fields as harmonics or astronomy generally rejected his recommendations for a purely a priori attack on those subjects. Even harmonic theorists who argued that it was the properties of numbers themselves that determined concords accepted that they needed to study musical sounds (Barker 1989). No subsequent practising Greek astronomer accepted the injunction to 'leave the things in the heavens alone', even though differing views were taken about the status of the observable data.

But then, second, there were those who argued that Plato was quite mistaken on the nature of mathematics and its objects themselves. The first to do so was his pupil Aristotle and this takes me to our next rich source of Greek materials for our study.

Aristotle's philosophy of mathematics has been variously interpreted but it is now generally accepted that it marks a radical departure from Plato (Lear 1982). For Plato, as we have seen, the objects of mathematics are separately existing intelligible objects, differing from the Forms on the one hand and from perceptible particulars on the other. But for Aristotle what mathematics studies is not such independently existing intelligibles, but rather the mathematical properties of perceptible phenomena. It does so by abstracting from other characteristics of those phenomena, their colour or their temperature, for instance. But its focus nevertheless is on properties that belong to and are exemplified by perceptible phenomena and that do not exist in isolation from them.

Analogously, where Plato had insisted on the independent existence of the intelligible Forms, for Aristotle what primarily exists independently are individual substances, such as this human being, or that horse, each of which consists of a combination of form and matter. That immediately reverses Plato's view of where attention should be focused. This should no longer be on independently existing Forms, but rather on the form–matter combinations of the concrete objects of experience. Their intelligibility was not a matter of participating in or imitating a Form, for intelligible forms are now instantiated in composites, not separate from them. Thus to suggest that physical substances should be analysed in basically quantitative, mathematical terms in any of the versions of atomism with which Aristotle is familiar, is, he would say, to commit a category mistake. The essentially qualitative properties of physical objects, their being hot, cold, wet, and dry and so on, are not to be reduced to quantitative differentiae, a move that thereby sees off atomism whether in its Democritean or its Platonic mode. The four simple bodies, Fire, Air, Water, and Earth can be analysed in terms of combinations of those four primary qualities, fire being hot and dry, air hot and 'wet',[11] and so on, but any further reductive analysis is ruled out.

That might look as if it torpedoed Plato's whole programme of a certain mathematization of physics (to use quite anachronistic terminology) but once again that does not give us the whole story. While not himself engaging in what he called the mathematical branches of physics, harmonics, astronomy, optics, and mechanics, Aristotle nevertheless broadly endorsed the ways in which each of them used mathematics in their study.

The point is clearest in the case of the study of the heavens. In his most notable foray in that field, in book Lambda of the *Metaphysics*, Aristotle reports the theories of the astronomers Eudoxus and Callippus and adds to them on his own account. How far and at what points this work drew on near Eastern investigations is controversial.[12] Aristotle evidently knew of both Egyptian and Babylonian data and even cites observations going back hundreds of years in support of his claim that the heavens are unchanging (*On the Heavens* 270b13ff.). Yet the agenda that Eudoxus and Callippus set themselves is original: it had no ancient near Eastern precedent. The chief problem was to see how the apparently irregular movements of the sun, moon and planets could be given a geometrical explanation, that is seen to be the resultant of the combination of certain perfectly regular circular movements.

For this purpose first Eudoxus and then Callippus postulated a certain number of concentric spheres, which were successful, at least in qualitative terms, in showing how irregularities could be so reduced, though the actual number of spheres needed remained disputed and our

[11] The Greek terms for 'wet' and 'dry' are *hugron* and *xēron*, where the contrast at stake is sometimes that between liquids or fluids and solids.
[12] I expressed my view on the subject in Lloyd 1996b: ch. 8. But compare, for example, Evans 1998, Bowen 2001, and 2002.

reconstruction of their solutions is stymied by a lack of reliable detailed information. But Aristotle's contribution was to deal with the interrelations of these spheres. To prevent the movement of a higher sphere being affected by those below it, he introduced retroactive spheres to cancel out the lower movements. This gave the whole system a concrete physical interpretation, though it should be stressed that Aristotle expresses great hesitancy about the actual number of spheres that will be needed.

His conviction that the whole forms a single coherent system is apparent, even though what that system was made of was not the four elements we see around us on earth but rather a fifth element, *aithēr*, which has the property of moving eternally in a circle, and of being neither hot nor cold, neither dry nor wet. This introduction of a gulf between the so-called sublunary sphere and the heavens themselves has often been condemned as a disaster for astronomy. But to that it must be said that Aristotle thought the conclusion was forced on him by the apparently unchanging circular motion of the heavens which, as noted, he believed to have been established by observations carried out by Egyptians and Babylonians as well as by his own Greek predecessors. That movement could not be forced, for then it would not be eternal and unchanging. But if it is natural, it could not be explained in terms of the natural movements of heavy bodies towards the centre of the earth (deemed to coincide with the centre of the universe) or of light ones away from that centre. The irony has often been pointed out that, when judged—anachronistically—from the standpoint of later dynamics, the trouble with Aristotle's account of motion was not excessive abstraction in the case of the fifth element, but rather insufficient abstraction from the effects we would put down to friction in the case of the sublunary ones.

Aristotle was of course more at home in the detailed study of animals than in any of the various branches of mathematics. Yet as we saw he developed an original philosophy of mathematics that served to deflate some of the more extravagant claims made for its study. More positively there was his contribution, already noted, to the development of the concept of axiomatic–deductive proof. In the *Posterior Analytics*, as I mentioned, he points out that the primary propositions on which deductions depend, axioms, definitions, and hypotheses, must themselves be self-evident, else they would need to be themselves demonstrated and so would not be primary. With those secure, valid deductive inferences will establish not just the truth but also the certainty and necessity of the conclusions. How far any previous mathematician had progressed towards such an explicit concept is controversial. On the one hand, most of Aristotle's actual examples in that book are mathematical. On the other, not all are and he evidently considered that the model of demonstration he thereby made explicit was applicable in other domains besides the mathematical. I shall come back later to some of the difficulties of that extension.

After Aristotle several bifurcations in the fortunes of the mathematical sciences take place among the Greeks. On the one hand, the first more or less complete systematization of most available mathematical knowledge was the achievement of Euclid, drawing no doubt heavily on the studies of his predecessors. Whether or not he was aware of Aristotle's *Posterior Analytics*, the *Elements* follows the model of demonstration it provides on the whole fairly closely. However, his primary indemonstrables differ from Aristotle's notably in that they now include postulates, especially the parallel postulate which is the fundamental assumption on which his geometry is based. This states that non-parallel straight lines meet at a point, though some later mathematicians thought that that had no business among the postulates but was rather a theorem that should be proved. As is well known, the successive attempts to demonstrate it were eventually, in the seventeenth century, to lead to the development of non-Euclidean geometries.

But aside from this ambition at systematization, impressive original work in a variety of branches of mathematics was achieved by both Apollonius of Perge (studying conic sections) and even more especially by Archimedes himself, not just in fairly elementary works such as *On the Sphere and Cylinder*, but in such advanced studies as *On Spirals* and *On the Quadrature of the Parabola* (Netz 2017). In Archimedes we see the power of Greek mathematical proof both in what we should call pure mathematics and in applied, that is in such fields as statics and hydrostatics. Given that he is able to build on Euclid's results, he does not need to set out all his axioms. But rigorous deductive proof is very much the ideal. Even when, as in the *Method*, he is prepared to develop less strict methods in the services of heuristics, the results discovered have thereafter to be made the subject of rigorous demonstration.

Yet to get these famous developments into proper perspective several qualifications need to be added. First, it is far from the case that every Greek mathematician was intent on producing demonstrations on that Euclidean model.[13] Plenty of work evidenced in the writings of Hero of Alexandria in the first century CE in particular has no such ambition (Cuomo 2001). The traditions of the attack on problems of mensuration that go back to the Greeks' near Eastern neighbours continue throughout the Mediterranean area and throughout all periods of antiquity (Høyrup 1994). An interest in mechanical devices, some of practical use such as the crane and the pulley, some just for show or entertainment, like automata, is also widely attested. Interestingly enough, although Hero makes no bid for the intellectual superiority of his investigations, he claims that they are better than traditional 'philosophy' at securing peace of mind. Simplifying drastically, his view is that if you want to be free from anxiety—as the philosophers repeatedly insisted—what you needed was not some philosophical theory about the *Summum Bonum*, but rather better weaponry than your opponents. That was to be achieved not by adopting some philosophical doctrine, but by the sustained study and application of mechanics (Tybjerg 2004).

But then the second qualification that needs to be made relates to the way in which the applicability of axiomatic–deductive model of demonstration was exaggerated. Already in Aristotle there is a question mark as to whether or how far it was indeed relevant to most branches of the study of natural phenomena (Lloyd 1996b). But when we turn to the second century CE physician and philosopher Galen, we can see that his attempts to provide axiomatic proofs in the study of what we would call the physiology of the human body or its pathology were quite misleading (Lloyd 2006, cf. Barnes 1991, Hankinson 1991). Among the self-evident axioms that he recognized was the principle that nature does nothing in vain. But so far from being self-evident, this was highly controversial. A second principle was that 'opposites are cures for opposites', but everything there depended on what counted as an opposite, and to have the principle come out true tended to make it vacuous. A third was that nothing happens without a cause. But even that had been denied

---

[13] Indeed Archimedes himself was not always concerned with such demonstrations for he had developed interests also in the field we should call combinatorics.

by the Epicureans who to secure free will imagined that some events (the swerve) are uncaused. Of course, Galen would have protested that such a doctrine was unsustainable and deeply mistaken. But that does not alter the point that so far from being a self-evident truth, this principle was hotly contested. The claim for its self-evidence had to rely on an assumption that that controversy could be definitively settled.

Galen thus provides one example where the bid to adopt a basically mathematical model of proof in other areas of science led to considerable difficulties. Let me jump ahead now to the fifth century CE to consider an even more striking example, namely Proclus' attempt to do the same in the realm of theology. Proclus was responsible for a history of mathematics, which is our main source for those whose writings themselves are not extant. He repeats the common Greek belief that geometry originated in Egypt, arising from the need to cope with the problems of land measurement caused by the flooding of the Nile. But his view of the role of Euclid is that the *Elements* was geared all along to solving the problem eventually tackled in book 13, namely the construction of the five regular solids that Plato had drawn attention to. For Proclus Euclid is a Platonist, through and through. Then in Proclus' own *Elements of Theology* we find what purports to be a Euclidean systematization of theories of the divine, proceeding from indemonstrable primary propositions to the proof of such doctrines as the benevolence of God. The ideal of axiomatic–deductive demonstration, which was absent from other ancient traditions of mathematics, proved something of a mirage for some Greek endeavours to secure incontrovertibility for their world-views.

By Proclus' time, in the fifth century CE, revived versions of what passed as Platonism and as Pythagoreanism had had several periods of fashion at least in some quarters. At the turn of the third and fourth centuries CE the neo-Pythagorean Iamblichus shows how far some were prepared to go. In his *On the Common Mathematical Science* he develops an extreme version of the notion that mathematics is the key to science, invoking the Pythagoreans as ancient authorities for just such a view (cf. Sambursky 1962: 47ff.).

The Pythagoreans, he says (ch. 23), valued mathematics and applied it in many different ways to the study of the cosmos. 'They considered what is possible and impossible in the structure of the universe on the basis of what is possible and impossible in mathematics, and they apprehended the celestial revolutions with their causes according to commensurate numbers'. Mathematics, in fact, he goes on to say (ch. 32), enables one to understand not just the movements of the heavenly bodies, but many other natural phenomena as well:

> It is also the custom of mathematics sometimes to attack mathematically perceptible things as well, such as the four elements, by using geometry or arithmetic or harmonics, and similarly with other matters. For since mathematics is prior in nature, and is derived from principles that are prior to those of natural objects, for that reason it constructs its demonstrative syllogisms from causes that are prior ... Thus I think we attack mathematically everything in nature and in the world of coming-to-be.

With Iamblichus we reach, as I said, an extreme exemplified by his use of mathematics in the service of theurgy, that is to bend the divine to your will. But we have one final set of examples to consider to illustrate both the powers of a programme of mathematical study and the difficulties its implementation faced. This will enable me to return to territory that is more familiar to us. I refer to the impressive corpus of works of Ptolemy in the second century CE, that spanned astronomy, harmonics, optics, and geography. In each case he drew extensively, naturally enough, on earlier work, including detailed records of Babylonian observations that go all the way back to the first year in the reign of Nabonassar (747 BCE). At the same time, his own original contributions were considerable and proved to be enormously influential.

At the outset of his astronomical masterpiece, which he named the *Mathematical Composition* (*Syntaxis*, or *Almagest* as it came to be known), he positions mathematical astronomy in relation to both 'physics' and 'theology'. By 'physics' he understands the study of the world of change in the sublunary sphere and by 'theology' the study of god, conceived as invisible and unchanging. 'Mathematics', that is the mathematical study of the heavens that he is about to embark on, is superior, he claims, to both those other two. Both of those are matters of conjecture rather than of scientific understanding, theology because of its utter obscurity, and physics because of the instability of its subject-matter. 'Mathematics' alone yields unshakeable knowledge, precisely because it does so by means of indisputable arithmetic and geometric demonstrations.

Here too then we find the theme we have become used to in Greece, namely that the great strength of the mathematical sciences lies in their capacity to deliver proof and certainty. Ptolemy does not set out his axioms in Aristotelian or Euclidean style, although he is at pains to justify his main assumptions, including that of the sphericity of the heavens, and the sphericity of the earth, as well as the doctrine that it is at rest in the centre of the universe, in the opening book of the treatise. But it is thanks to its use of mathematical procedures that astronomy occupies the preeminent place it does in human intellectual disciplines.

But there is more. In the very first chapter of the work we have a text that sets out in the clearest possible terms the wider ambitions of the study of the heavens, not merely intellectual but also cosmological and moral ones. Mathematical astronomy does not just give us knowledge and understanding but leads to an appreciation of the beauty and order of the heavens. Then he has this to say about its influence on human character (*Syntaxis* I 1, H I 7.17ff):

> Of all studies this one especially would prepare humans to be percep-
> tive of nobility both of action and of character. When the sameness,
> good order, proportion and freedom from arrogance of divine things
> are being contemplated, this study makes those who follow it lovers of
> this divine beauty, and instils, and as it were makes natural, the same
> condition in their soul.

The moral implications of the study of the heavens are given another twist when he considers the status of that other main branch of the subject, namely astrology, in his *Tetrabiblos*. The aim of astrology, like that of astronomy itself, is predictive, but its predictions relate not to the unchanging movements in the heavens, but to events on earth, and the problem here is that 'every study that deals with the quality of matter is conjectural'. Indeed Ptolemy dismisses much earlier work, including the schemata that he attributes to the 'Chaldeans', as unsound and yet he holds that predictions about events on earth are possible, even if always a matter of conjecture. Moreover this study too can be justified on the grounds of its contribution to well-being, in that it enables humans to face the future with calm and steadiness (*Tetrabiblos* I ch. 2) since they would be armed with foreknowledge of what was to come. That must be said to be fanciful, for it would depend on the predictions made being more accurate than they could reasonably be claimed to be.

The programme that Ptolemy outlines for mathematical astronomy is absolutely clear: it aims to provide indisputable demonstrations of the movements of the sun, moon, and planets. But how far, we must ask, was such a programme achieved in practice? The geometry of the construction of his models is crystal clear. Yet the parameters that have to be used in their application to each of the heavenly bodies studied are extremely complex. The main periods of revolution in every case, as determined by sustained observations going back to the Babylonians, do not correspond to values expressible in simple numbers. On many occasions to allow the argument to proceed Ptolemy allows himself approximations. This applies in particular to the value he gave to the precession of the equinoxes, which he chooses to represent as 1° in 100 years, when the data on which he based that in *Syntaxis* VII ch. 2 suggest that that should have been taken as a lower value rather than the mean.

Then to get a better fit between data and geometrical models he has to complexify the latter. Neither a simple eccentric model, nor an epicyclic one, will do. So they have to be combined and indeed in some cases he has to have recourse to a further complicating element, the introduction of what came to be called the equant point. For each of the planets, the heavenly body moves on an epicyclic circle, the centre of which itself

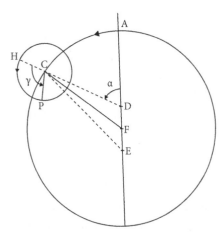

Fig. 8.1 Ptolemy's model for the planets other than Mercury.

moves round an eccentric circle (the 'deferent'). But the movement is uniform not with respect to the centre of the deferent, nor with respect to the centre of the ecliptic (the earth) but in relation to the equant point, which, for all the planets except Mercury, is a point on a line from the earth through the centre of the deferent and at the same distance from that centre as that centre is from the earth (see Fig. 8.1).[14]

For Mercury the added complication is that the centre of the deferent itself moves round the circumference of a circle whose centre is the equant point (see Fig. 8.2).[15]

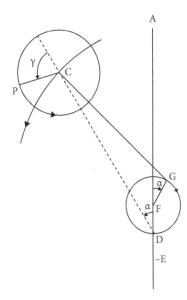

Fig. 8.2 Ptolemy's model for Mercury.

[14] *Syntaxis* IX 6. In Fig. 8.1 (Ptolemy's model for the planets other than Mercury) the planet P moves on the circumference of the epicycle centre C. C moves round an eccentric circle (called the deferent) with centre F, but the movement is uniform not with respect to F, nor with respect to E (the centre of the ecliptic, i.e. the earth) but with respect to point D, the 'equant'. The angle *a* increases uniformly. The equant is a point on the line from E to F such that FD equals EF.

[15] The added complication in the model for Mercury (Fig. 8.2) is that G, the centre of the deferent, itself moves round F at the same speed as, but in the opposite sense to, the motion of C on the deferent circle, measured with respect to D, the equant point. So while for the other planets the centre of the deferent is the midpoint of the line joining the earth to the equant, for Mercury the equant is the midpoint between the earth and the centre of the circle round which the centre of the deferent revolves. Cf. Neugebauer 1975, I: 162.

Of course the introduction of the equant was later to be greeted with derision, for it seemed quite arbitrary and to have no physical correlate, though Ptolemy insisted that some such complexification was necessary to fit the extensive observational data available to him. Yet complex though the models were, they enabled remarkably accurate predictions of the movements of the planets to be made, and the *Handy Tables* that set out their cycles continued to be usable for centuries after Ptolemy's death. However, from time to time Ptolemy's own sense of the difficulties he faced surfaces in the *Syntaxis* itself. Thus when he comes to consider movements in latitude (north and south of the ecliptic) he has this to say (*Syntaxis* XIII ch. 2, H II 532.12ff., Toomer 1984: 600):

> Let no one, considering the complicated nature of our devices, judge such hypotheses to be over-elaborated. For it is not appropriate to compare human [constructions] with divine, nor to form one's beliefs about such great things on the basis of very dissimilar analogies...
> Rather, one should try, as far as possible, to fit the simpler hypotheses to the heavenly movements, but if this does not succeed, [one should apply hypotheses] which do fit.

We have to assume that the heavens are simple, even though they may not seem so to us. We have, in other words, to invoke a quite different notion of 'simplicity'. Here it is no longer a methodological principle to decide between competing models, but an a priori postulate. The movements of the heavenly bodies *must* be 'simple', however complex they may appear to us.

We are evidently a far cry from the optimistic claims in the first book, that the study of the 'good order' and 'freedom from arrogance' of heavenly movements will enable us to achieve good order in our own souls. But despite the difficulties he faced, in the complexity of the models and in achieving a fit with the observational data, Ptolemy remains unmoved in his faith that mathematics provides the key to the understanding of the cosmos and beyond that to our own self-fulfilment.

*   *   *

My survey of just some of the extensive materials for the study of ancient Chinese and Greek mathematical ideas and practices has necessarily been highly selective, and my use of modern ethnographic data has been even more cursory. Yet it has already brought to light a striking heterogeneity in the answers given or presupposed to the five questions that I posed at the outset, concerning the objects of mathematics, the relations between its various branches, the knowledge it yields and how that is to be acquired, and its relevance to an understanding of natural phenomena—and notably its contribution to human happiness and well-being. Nor if we turn to our own mathematics can we say that the problems have now all been resolved to everyone's satisfaction. It is true that certain preoccupations now figure less prominently in the work of modern professional mathematicians. While many share the ambition we find in the *Zhoubi suanjing* and in Plato, among many others, that mathematics can somehow provide the key to the understanding of the universe, they are generally less concerned to pay attention to the symbolic associations of numbers or shapes. Yet on the basic questions of the nature of the objects studied, and the status of the knowledge it yields, very different answers are still being given by intuitionists, by Platonists, by constructivists, formalists, and logicists (cf. Hacking 2014).

But all this heterogeneity and disagreement lead us inevitably to pose the fundamental issue of whether there is any justification for thinking of mathematics as a unified discipline at all. When we encounter startlingly divergent beliefs and practices implied or made explicit in different ancient or modern groups of people, is it a mistake to appeal to a unifying concept of mathematics in interpretation? Does not the heterogeneity suggest that we should resist the temptation to ask what their 'mathematics' consists in as if that were a correct diagnosis of their concerns, especially when, as in many indigenous societies, the actors in question have no such overarching concept themselves?

Several mistakes lie in wait for the unwary here. The first is to assess other notions and practices by the light of whatever we take to be the best modern Western mathematical understanding. That commits two types of errors, the first being that it downplays those ongoing disputes within modern mathematics that I have just mentioned. The second relates to the general methodological principle of not imposing our categories (whatever they may be) in interpreting those of other groups, as if we somehow had a monopoly of the truth.

But the converse second generic kind of mistake is to respond to the heterogeneity by concluding that the data in question are strictly incomparable. That is to go from a recognition of incommensurability to an inference of unintelligibility, a move that I have criticized elsewhere in these investigations. If, on the one hand, we see the danger of assuming a simple, totally unified and homogeneous field of cognitive endeavour, at the opposite extreme, we have to avoid the mistake of taking it that there are simply no commonalities in the ideas and practices we are dealing with. That obliges us to say, to be sure, what those commonalities are, but that can be answered at least provisionally. We may do so in terms of an appreciation, some appreciation, first of number or at least of quantity, and, second, of shapes and forms and of how they may be combined, manipulated, and transformed. For all the differences in the counting systems, or in the conception of number that is used, for all the different values associated with number, they all share a basic recognition of plurality, that is some mode of plurality howsoever understood. Again, for all the differences in the nature or degree of interests in the exploration of shapes and forms, they all manifest a recognition that such magnitudes can be distinguished and investigated, manipulated, and used.

No doubt some might protest that what is interesting about what ancient and modern societies have made of numbers and shapes is rather the diversity that we uncover, the different ways in which all of that relates to views about the world we live in and even of humans' places in it, the interaction between 'mathematics' and cosmology and even ethics. I would agree both as to the fact of that diversity and to the interest in pursuing the factors that contributed to it. But I would add that that should not be at the cost of losing sight of the underlying commonalities. Within the limits and reservations we have discussed, we may say that that diversity bears witness to a basic cluster of cognitive capacities that humans—and also to some extent some other species of animals— possess. Whether a similar analysis and analogous conclusion apply to other areas of cognitive experience remains to be investigated. I turn next to religion.

9

Test Case 2

Religion

As noted already in Chapter 3, one reason for us to be especially wary in our discussion of religion lies in the role that concept once played in naive positivistic theories of the development of human rationality. Those speculations had it that religion was to be contrasted on the one hand with magic and superstition, on the other with science and philosophy. Some argued that it superseded the former pair. Where science was concerned some held that it was perfectly compatible with religion, while others have put it that with the advance of science most religious beliefs in turn should be seen to be deluded (e.g. Dawkins 2006). The first problem with any such developmental theories is that they focus just on belief and on the criterion of truth or falsity, thereby downplaying the role of behaviour and practice. The second is that they ignore the continued presence of magic and superstition in any society, however civilized it might claim itself to be.

The chief issues we must confront here are of three distinct but interlocking kinds. First and most obviously, it is anything but clear what we mean by 'religion'. That question is not to be settled by appeal to dictionary definitions, even though they are, of course, suggestive, for they offer conflicting advice. Rather we have to go back to some basic data, linguistic, psychological, and sociological. They include first the range of usages of the English term and of other terms in other languages that have been thought, with greater or less justification, to be approximately equivalent. Thus the Latin term from which our own is derived, *religio*, has distinct pejorative undertones, often being equivalent to what we would label superstition. But evidently we should not restrict our inquiry to societies that have some such explicit term. While the dangers of being overinfluenced by familiar features of modern Western society

Intelligence and Intelligibility: Cross-Cultural Studies of Human Cognitive Experience. G. E. R. Lloyd, Oxford University Press (2020). © G. E. R. Lloyd.
DOI: 10.1093/oso/9780198854593.001.0001

are obvious, we should not limit what can be considered to be religious phenomena to what is found in complex (and not just Western) cultures on the grounds that what is reported from indigenous communities lacks coherence, a body of doctrine and standardized religious services, for instance (Boyer and Baumard 2018, cf. Barrett 2000). We have, to be sure, to start with some inkling of what the religious domain comprises, even while, as usual, we must be prepared to revise our understanding as the investigation proceeds and even in the end admit that in some respects a fully adequate general account of the phenomena remains beyond our reach.

Second, even if we can settle, provisionally, on some understanding of the kinds of beliefs and practices in question, we confront the question of whether or how far some such are shared by all humans. This is the principal issue we are focusing on here, of whether we are indeed dealing with a cross-cultural universal, or with phenomena that are essentially culturally specific and that may or may not be exemplified in any given human group or by any individual. Does whatever we count as religion correspond to some universal human biological, psychological, or social need, or arise merely in contingent particular circumstances? Is religion in any sense a 'natural' phenomenon, for example in that it depends on non-cultural properties of the human mind (Boyer 1994)? Caution is evidently particularly needed at this juncture, in part because of the great importance that religion—any religion—may play in the lives of those who believe and practise it. But that special role does not, of course, by itself justify any positive conclusion on the issue of religion's universality.

Third, we must ask how far mutual understanding between individuals or groups is attainable in this domain, and how and by whom that is to be assessed. The more we have to recognize difficulties and obstacles, the greater the repercussions for our inquiry into the first two questions. If and when we find mutual understanding breaks down, we have to reconsider whether we are dealing with the same type of phenomena or experience, and that will certainly impact on our conclusions on the second question, of whether whatever we count as religion is shared by all humans.

On the first definitional issue, for many what is at stake is no mere intellectual matter but their well-being, happiness, salvation. Surveying what others have held on the question, we are faced with a plethora of views, some quite complex, others attempting to identify some basic human capacity, feeling or need. Do all humans share in some such (my second question), whether or not they acknowledge that? Some monotheisms claim there is only one religion, and other systems of belief and ritual are not religions at all (cf. Chapter 1 on the rites controversy in China). But others distinguish between the one true religion and false imitations, allowing the latter the status of religion even while condemning them as deeply mistaken, maybe the work of the devil. Thus much hangs on the answer to the main problem we are investigating in this set of studies, concerning what all humans do or do not have in common.

Among those who have grappled with the problem, Geertz, in a famous essay, offered a five-part definition and an extended commentary on that (Geertz 1973: 90ff.). For him, religion is '(1) a system of symbols which acts to (2) establish powerful, pervasive and long-lasting moods and motivations in men by (3) formulating conceptions of a general order of existence and (4) clothing these conceptions with such an aura of factuality that (5) the moods and motivations seem uniquely realistic'. That sets the bar quite high and implies an exceptional degree of explicitness. Other interpreters have taken very different views. Horton, in an essay criticizing Durkheim's theory of religion as derived from human social relations, put it that 'religion can be looked upon as an extension of the field of people's social relationships beyond the confines of purely human society', though in such an extension humans see themselves as 'dependent on their non-human alters' (Horton 1960: 211). However, if we go back to Tylor (1891: i: 424) religion was, on a minimal definition, a matter simply of a 'belief in Spiritual Beings' (cf. Goody 1961, Bloch 2008).

The scope for confusion is considerable. Some focus on institutions, rituals, or special personnel (priests, prophets, shamans) who are in charge of these and may have a right or a duty to interpret sacred texts or traditions about what is to be believed and how people should conduct themselves. There is, as noted, an obvious contrast between defining religion in terms of beliefs on the one hand, or of practices on the other. For some interpreters and some faithful, correct performance of ritual is crucial, for others doctrine is key, for yet others mood or emotion or a sense of awe is (Meyer 2016). Some may focus on a sense of what transcends merely human capabilities (Norenzayan 2013), while others may register the covert ideological underpinning of human social relations, and that is before we get to Marx's dictum, that religion is the opium of the masses, designed to hoodwink them and divert their attention from the class struggle.

Thus some favour sociological explanations, others psychological ones, for example, in terms of cognitive capacities or constraints. A recognized priesthood, set places of worship, a sacred text, solemn rituals, the practice of prayer and meditation, a belief in the afterlife, may all have claims to be marks of religious experience. But the possible circularity in many such formulations is obvious, in the use of those very terms 'priesthood', 'worship', and 'sacred' themselves. Moreover while some would deem some of the items we have mentioned as sufficient conditions for a phenomenon to count as 'religious', none seems a necessary condition for such to be the case. Some religions that we can recognize as such have no officiants, no holy texts, no set places of worship, even no god. Nor do all 'rituals' and 'prayers' invoke some idea of divinity. Social life is full of ceremonies that have nothing to do with any godhead. When we pray for some outcome, we often pin our hopes on human, not any divine, intervention.

On the other hand, just to appeal to some vague idea of spirituality is open to the opposite objection of being far too loose to ground concrete claims for universality, or rather the universality has been bought at the price of desperate indeterminacy. The same also applies to any appeal to some powers or forces other than, and stronger than, mere human ones. Those who recognize no god, and subscribe to no organized, institutionalized, faith, may still be awestruck by the power of an earthquake or a tsunami or a nuclear explosion without thinking of those in religious terms at all.

In a field that is so controversial and in which so much is thought by so many to be at stake, it would be foolish to think that we shall be able to resolve even a modicum of the outstanding problems at all adequately, let alone to everyone's satisfaction. But if we concentrate, as we do here, on the question of human uniformities and diversities, one line of investigation seems promising at least at first sight. Boyer (1994, 2001) has drawn attention to one recurrent feature, namely the combination of common-or-garden beliefs—to do with agents, motives, more or less transparent cause–effect relations—and moderately counter-intuitive ones (cf. Pyysiainen 2001, Pyysiainen and Anttonen 2002, Atran 2002, Luhrmann 2020). The counter-intuitive suggestions attract attention and demand explanation, and in Boyer's view the particular modes of account likely to be favoured draw on causal understandings that are deeply rooted in human psychology. Anthropomorphism, he argues (Boyer 1996 and cf. Guthrie 1993, Barrett and Keil 1996, Daston and Mitman 2005), is natural in the sense that it corresponds to basic cognitive constraints that can be confirmed by cross-cultural studies of children's psychological development.[1]

Moreover, where adults are concerned, competence in the mastery of the special vocabulary and concepts that go with religious belief may take a very different form from the acquisition of ordinary language skills. This has been discussed under the rubric of 'empty concepts' (Boyer 1986, cf. Keane 1997) sometimes exemplified by 'mana' or 'tabu' (taboo) for instance. The claim is that these are not learnt by accessing new meanings, so much as by the recognition of their usage in context, irrespective of any content, for on that score they may be devoid of any—though that would be hard to claim for 'mana' and 'tabu' themselves.

Counter-intuitiveness may be even more prominent. God's being everywhere is understood in terms of the common perception of any ordinary object being somewhere, while that understanding depends on an appreciation of difference as well as of similarity. God's being omnipresent in the world is very different from the way an ordinary human exists in space, though 'omnipresent' implies spatial location. Our being in a particular place rules out our being in any other, but that restriction does not apply to the deity. Again His being omnipotent draws on our sense of ordinary persons having some limited power or capacity, even though the difference is that His is unlimited.

---

[1] As I shall be noting shortly, one problem with any overarching theory of the cognitive demands to which religion offers an answer is to say how it is that not every society, let alone every individual, signs up to the same solution to the problem, not just to the same specific set of religious beliefs and practices, but to any that can be said to fall under that rubric. It is not just in societies that have influential literate elites that certain religious ideas and practices come to be challenged—as I charted for ancient Greece in Lloyd 1979: ch. 1. For as has often been documented, there is plenty of evidence from indigenous mainly oral communities of the possibility for the expression of scepticism about all aspects of traditional lore and concerning the authority of those who purport to be its custodians.

The underlying idea here may be thought to owe something to much earlier observations by Durkheim and others on the contrast between the 'sacred' and the 'profane'. The latter covers the ordinary, the mundane, while the sacred stands in contrast to that, whether with a positive valence (holy) or with a negative one (maybe the work of the devil). That distinction derives from the contrast between the two terms 'sacer' and 'profanus' in Latin, but is certainly not confined to languages and cultures that have some connection with those with Indo-European roots. Some sense of the difference between the ordinary and the extra-ordinary may be very common, perhaps universal, but first, ideas of what is ordinary may differ widely, and second, perception of what is out of the ordinary does not, as we said, necessarily go with the idea that divine or spiritual forces are at work. The universalizing tendencies in any thesis as to the naturalness of religion allow, one may say, too little scope for the variety of responses to the uncommon or the puzzling that can be attested. If fundamental cognitive constraints are indeed at work, we would expect greater uniformity in their expression.

However, the idea that religious belief may fill some cognitive shortfall is worth pursuing further, in particular in the light of the fact that a tension arises when such belief may itself be a source of cognitive dissonance. Recourse to divine intervention may resolve one difficulty, that of explaining the apparently extraordinary phenomenon or event, only to raise one further back in the causal chain. For that intervention demands that belief in the ordinary rules of cause and effect is suspended. Yet so far from undermining the credibility of the appeal to the divine, the appreciation of its totally exceptional character may even reinforce its attractiveness at least to some.

As I have argued elsewhere (Lloyd 2009: 152) the counter-intuitive elements in religious belief and practice are both a strength and a weakness. On the one hand, the totally exceptional nature of the godhead is one feature that increases the sense, among the faithful, that the religion is worth adhering to. On the other, that very exceptionality imposes a constant pressure on its credibility and constitutes an inherent potential source of vulnerability to challenge. Participation in belief has to become routinized for the evident paradoxes on which it depends not to cause more cognitive dissonance than it resolves (cf. Whitehouse 2000, 2004). Not all religious beliefs have elites to defend their positions in the face of criticisms and objections—elites that maintain their authority partly by their ability, real or imagined, to counter such threats. But with or without such elites to do the explaining, the paradox is that the very questionability of a set of beliefs may be turned into a source of unquestionability. Yet some may resist any such move and conclude that the costs in terms of cognitive dissonance outweigh the benefits.

We face here something of a crux. An old-fashioned positivist view would have it that religion, any religion, promotes social cohesion and provides solace in the face of misfortune, especially death. A latter-day version of that would identify that as yielding an evolutionary advantage for human sociality.[2] Yet if it does so, it achieves that at a price. It could hardly be claimed by even the most ardent advocate of such a view that adherence to a religion always promotes the well-being of the group in question, even as that is understood by the members of that group. That type of functionalist interpretation just cannot be sustained. To start with, the economic cost of ritual observances, of maintaining priesthoods and constructing suitable places for worship is never zero and can be exorbitantly high, even if those sites do not have to be as grand as Chartres cathedral or Stonehenge. If one of the injunctions of many monotheistic faiths is that the unfaithful need to be converted and their souls saved, that may involve aggressive behaviour—conquest and suppression—that can be costly, even if the appropriation of the infidels' goods and property has so often been used to defray those expenses. Some have argued that warfare, which is such a pervasive phenomenon in human history, including those conducted with a view to propagating the one true faith, is ultimately advantageous to human development, as stimulating innovation (cf. Hinde 1992). But the destruction it entails makes the cost–benefit analysis anything but straightforward. Besides, the advantage, if there is one, in terms of innovation, corresponds to nothing in the intentions of the participants.

Against that, others would argue that even if aggression may be necessary for survival in the jungle or the savannah, it represents an instinct that complex polities would do well to bring under control, if not

---

[2] This is an argument developed with due caution and tentativeness by Dennett (2006: 9). His book ends (2006: 314) by listing the as yet unresolved empirical questions the study of religion faces. Others who have made much of the role of religion in securing social adhesion include Boyer and Baumard 2018, cf. Barrett 2000, Atran 2002, Bellah 2011.

to suppress entirely. But some would supplement that consideration with the suggestion that religion is an effective way of sublimating such urges, though the trouble with that argument in turn is obvious. However much a religion may preach peace among all humankind, it may find itself needing to use stronger persuasive methods than mere words to establish its claim to superiority over other, heathen, beliefs.

In answer to the first of the questions I posed at the outset, no single simple definition of 'religion' is adequate to capture the heterogeneous beliefs and practices that have some claim to be included on the grounds that they invoke some aspects of the 'sacred', that is the divine, the spiritual, even, some might say, just the starkly exceptional. If we take such a generous, even permissive, view on the first question, that may be seen to increase the possibility that some of the phenomena in question are common to human groups across the board—which would provisionally give a positive answer to my second question. But we have seen that the first danger here is that of draining religion of all positive content and then the second is that if we restore content, the risk becomes one of downplaying the distinctiveness of the beliefs and practices that most would want to qualify as religion, let alone the different degrees to which they become institutionalized and as I put it routinized. When blocks to ordinary understanding occur, one evident common pattern of reaction is some recourse to extraordinary spiritual or supernatural causation. At the same time we need to recognize the variety of forms that any such appeal may take, and the diverse types of doubts and criticisms that may be expressed or registered as to whether leaving the ordinary behind is a sensible tactic in the face of uncertainty, puzzlement, misfortune, or the sense of hopelessness. Bearing that in mind, we can hardly claim that any such tactic is universally adopted across all human individuals and groups.

Our third question related to the issue of intelligibility. If appeal to religion is some response to the inexplicable, how can recourse to what seemingly breaks the rules help to keep those rules in place? How can the sacred be understood by the profane? How can a set of religious beliefs or practices be understood by those who do not adhere to them, but to some other set, or to none at all? Have not the answers we have offered to my first two questions bought the intelligibility of religions at the cost of stripping them of all their distinctive power and content?

To begin to tackle those issues we need to reintroduce both the social institutions within which religion is practised and the human agents who may be responsible for its, and their, preservation and interpretation. But first a caveat is in order, about the possibility of the effective denial of the social character of religion in the first place. Mystics are not always hermits in the desert. If some were, others, such as Teresa of Avila, were certainly important players in the political life of the communities to which they belonged. But the mystical experience as such, as James showed, is an intensely private one, to the point where the one thing that is communicated and communicable to others is just the fact that some exceptional experience has occurred, not any of the content of that experience. The mystic, like the solipsist, is to that extent beyond the reach of the outsider's understanding.

Yet more normally religions stop short of claiming they are beyond understanding, however much they may insist on the difficulty of attaining such understanding as is within reach. To be in a fit state even to begin some such progression will generally involve more than just intellectual preparation, for only those who have undergone the proper ritual purification, the appropriate initiation, may be accepted as supplicants for instruction. Crucially they must show devotion. Their role is not to question why these procedures must be adopted: it may even be a test of their eligibility that they accept without demur that that is how it must be, on the authority of the priests or elders who are taking them on. The key quality the initiates need to demonstrate is simply unquestioning faith.

In some instances that figure in the ethnographic reports the strain on the initiates' readiness to accept whatever they are taught is acute. Studying the Baktaman, Barth (1975) showed that there is not just one simple rite of passage but a sequence of six or seven. At each successive stage the initiate is taught that what was learned at the previous one is not just incomplete, but deeply flawed, morally unsound indeed. They discover, for example, that in an earlier rite they broke an important taboo, not just inadvertently, but under the instruction they were given. The whole sequence is under the control of elders, but only the most senior members of the society can have any confidence that there are no further surprises in store for them. The importance of ritual correctness is constantly underlined, only to be repeatedly undermined when the next level of understanding is introduced.

The issue that last remark raises is whether understanding is the object of the exercise, or one of them, in the first place. What is important, in most religions, is not intellectual comprehension, but sincere participation, communion, indeed, with the divine. What matters is that the ceremonies should be performed correctly, that is in the view of those responsible for leadership and guidance in the matter. The gap between ordinary behaviour (the profane) and heightened ritual (the sacred) may be recognized, but for the latter to work (to be efficacious or at least felicitous) adherence to due procedure is what counts, not access to some rationale or account, even one that draws on accepted modes of explanation. Elements of the mysterious are no obstacle to that felicity and may even contribute to it. However, as I noted in my earlier discussion of the contrast between efficacy and felicity, why certain behaviour is accepted as appropriate, under the second rubric, itself poses questions. How did it come to have that status and who is or was responsible for deciding that? Felicity, after all, can be as contentious as efficacy, or even more so.

If we allow, as we must, for the difficulty of delimiting what is to count as 'religious', that just increases one's sense of the problem of generalizing across cultures and periods. Some religious faiths, we said, admit others, while in some cases any such accommodation is prohibited. Some faiths have priests in positions of authority laying down what is to be believed and how to behave, while others make do without such, where spiritual life lacks any obvious institutional framework. That may leave as the bare minimum some sense of a contrast between the mundane and the sacred. When in the latter realm ordinary explanations fail, that serves to underscore that contrast, at the price, indeed, of simultaneously underscoring the limits of intelligibility of what belongs to the sacred. The outsider can and does register the exceptional nature of the behaviour, including the linguistic behaviour, the adherence to counter-intuitive articles of belief. The faithful, by contrast, may be not one bit abashed at the diagnosis of counter-intuitiveness, but accept that that merely emphasizes how special that faith is.

So the diversity in the actual beliefs and practices, and the difficulties of mutual intelligibility, are particularly pronounced in the religious sphere. We seem to have to settle for the observation that what remains common, across many if not all human groups, is some sense of the existence of some such sphere. While understanding of content may elude us, and often does, we have this much to go on, that the expectation is that the usual rules of interpretation have to be adapted or even suspended. In some instances the outsider may diagnose not just the mysterious, but deliberate mystification. But in others, mindful of how difficult it is to attain deep understanding, we may need to remind ourselves of the limits of our comprehension and of the need to probe further.

The conclusion of this brief study contrasts, therefore, with what I proposed at the end of our last inquiry, in Chapter 8, into mathematics. There I identified some sense of working with quantity, number, form, and shape as the basic commonality across human societies, even while the form the mathematical operations take, and the role they play in the value systems of the society in question, differ so widely. Where religion is concerned, an appreciably more sceptical conclusion is in order. We cannot reliably identify distinct cognitive capacities responsible for the diverse experiences that are in question. Thus we have expressed reservations about Boyer's claim that there are universal cognitive constraints at work and that in that sense religious experience is natural (cf. also Dennett 2006). Nor can that experience or rather those experiences be traced to features that are common to all humans in virtue of our biology or of our being the social animals we are. We all face death, to be sure, but do so in different ways, not necessarily pinning our hopes on an afterlife or on some benevolent deity who will ensure that all will be well with us, and the world, in the long run. We all depend on orderly social relations, but not necessarily ones that rely on divine sanction. We may agree that some sense of the extraordinary, even the spiritual, is common, but that too evokes different responses.

Religion, on that account, offers at most a supplementary but not necessary resource for dealing with the exceptional in human experience. It is one that carries its own cost in terms of credibility, where it may be as well for the outsider to recognize this not as a reason for swift dismissal, but rather as a challenge to our understanding. However, insofar as the sceptical conclusion holds, the task of investigating why particular beliefs and practices came to be developed at particular junctures becomes one for the cultural, social, and political historian, not one for the cognitive scientist. The fact is that religious beliefs and practices have continued in the modern world when some might have expected, some did expect, that they would wither and die out in the face of the increasing successes of science to explain the puzzling (cf. Hinde 1999). But we are not entitled to conclude from that persistence that religion—some religion—answers to a universal need, for that would be drastically to underestimate the contingent factors in the rise and fall of different sets of ideas and practices in different societies in different times and places, and the different degrees to which individuals or groups feel the need to have recourse to some notion of the divine or the spiritual to make sense of their experiences. In that regard the phenomena we classify under the generic rubric of religion pose problems that resist even the most determined efforts at a satisfactory general analysis.

10

Test Case 3

Law

Law has already figured on several occasions in our discussion. Some social groups have no codified legal system: indeed in many there is either no writing at all or only the most elementary forms of recording such as the aide-mémoires to which Goody (1977) drew attention. But of course that lack of a legal code does not prevent the prevailing customs or rules of behaviour from having force, even though both the means of implementing them, and the tactics that dissenters have to use to challenge them, may vary. Strathern's careful analysis of the situation in Papua New Guinea when indigenous tribes first came into contact with outsiders—government officials, missionaries, settlers, traders—is eloquent on the topic (Strathern 2019). The officials were convinced that to secure justice and good order, the law had to be codified, and the means for enforcing it had to be in place. But they came to recognize that indigenous customs had traditionally had great authority with the tribes in question, and so they accepted that they did have some standing, even in certain circumstances where they conflicted with the laws as newly codified. The pidgin term 'kastom' was used that served to convey that recognition, while at the same time it marked the difference between what indigenous peoples accepted and the—proper, regular—customs that the officials were used to.

The added complication that arises with large numbers of indigenous communities is that they do not share the basic notion of the individual as the locus of responsibility. Persons, in Strathern's graphic phrase, may be construed not so much as individuals as dividuals, where their agency fluctuates according to the varying relationships that govern a particular situation. So it is deeply mistaken to proceed on the assumption that

Intelligence and Intelligibility: Cross-Cultural Studies of Human Cognitive Experience. G. E. R. Lloyd, Oxford University Press (2020). © G. E. R. Lloyd.
DOI: 10.1093/oso/9780198854593.001.0001

good order in any society depends on having and using some equivalent to our concept of persons acting as just so many responsible individual moral agents. That evidently has widespread implications for the applicability of our notions of law insofar as they depend on the concept of individual responsibility, though, as we shall see, such reservations do not extend to a scepticism about the possibility of inquiring into ideas of morality itself.

Two further complications arise on the issue of responsibility. First, many societies, of which ancient China was one, have held that where a serious crime has been committed, it is not just the perpetrator who should be punished, but the whole extended family to which he or she belonged. On this conception, responsibility is corporate rather than individual. Second, the idea that responsibility is not limited to human agents is also well attested. In ancient Greece and in medieval Europe animals and even inanimate objects could be brought to trial for the parts they played in some act deemed to be criminal (Evans 1906).

Once the laws are written down, there is much less room for doubt about what they actually say, that is the legal provisions in force. This has been identified as a major factor in the development of Greek city-states (Gernet 1917, 1955, Vernant 1980, 1983). In principle, anyone who could read could verify for themselves what the laws contained, and even those who could not, knew that the laws were publicly accessible. Interestingly, in China the codification of the laws was sometimes deplored on the grounds that it deflected people's attention from the need to cultivate virtue.[1] And when legal systems were set up, many people complained of their complexity (*Han Shu* 23: 1101, Hulsewé 1955: 338, Lloyd 2009: 121).

Yet it was, and it still is, never the case that all ambiguity is removed. First, there was the question of the precise meaning of the terms of the laws themselves, and in addition to that there is the all-important issue of their applicability to any given case in dispute. Murder, the law may lay down, is to be punishable by death. But how is murder to be differentiated from other killings? Is killing in self-defence to count as murder? Killing by itself is not a sufficient condition, for otherwise legal execution will be murder. Then further doubts will arise concerning the particular

---

[1] That was a view ascribed to Confucius in the *Zuo Zhuan,* Zhao 29, cf. Graham 1989: 276, and a similar opinion is expressed in the *Daodejing* 57, associated with the legendary Laozi.

facts of the case in hand. A death has occurred. But why did that happen? Was some other individual involved? Who or what was to blame (in Greek the same group of terms, *aition*, *aitia*, and cognates, is used for blame and guilt and for causation more generally) and were there any mitigating circumstances? There may or may not be a rich vocabulary available to talk of diminished responsibility, modes of premeditation and intentionality and the like. But even without such linguistic resources the correct interpretation of what happened may be disputed and indeed whether there is a single unequivocal interpretation may be cast into doubt.

Possible challenges to the laws and customs, and to their implementation, are a key issue. In some societies there are clear procedures that govern the revision of the laws, while in others customs are subject to gradual, maybe imperceptible, changes corresponding to the changing situation within the society itself or in its external relations. At the opposite end of the spectrum, to challenge the law is to challenge the word of God. Those who present themselves as guardians of the law will claim not just that it is divinely sanctioned, but also that they themselves speak with god-given authority, whether or not they have a Sacred Text that purports to come direct from Heaven.

The dilemma that any legal system, formal or informal, faces is clear. On the one hand, the justification for the laws that is generally offered is that they are needed to secure good order in society: that is their *raison d'être*. For that to be achieved there has to be some way of enforcing what the laws or customs lay down, as that is interpreted either by the community as a whole or by some group within it. On the other hand, the imposition of punishments drives a wedge within society and is designed to inhibit if not to prevent certain individuals from behaving just as they like. In the name of the good of society as a whole, some of its members are to be treated, temporarily or permanently, as less than totally free agents. Jailing may be a temporary measure or long-lasting: exile or the deprivation of the rights of citizens or their status as full members of society may be permanent. Some are not stripped of their rights, so much as excluded from them from the outset by birth or by the social position they hold.

Of course other social animals besides humans have ways of dealing with deviants or individuals whom the group sees as a threat.

I mentioned before species of animals that have developed effective cheater detection mechanisms. But humans with language and complex social institutions possess particularly potent means of discussing and identifying the criteria of misbehaviour and of offering justifications both for how that is defined and for how it is to be dealt with. But the very fact that such matters can be made explicit opens up a certain possibility for the decisions to be challenged. The law is one thing, so the complaint will go, but justice is another. Those who principally benefit from the current arrangements will insist that they should not be changed, on pain of chaos breaking out. Those who are alert to that gap between legality and what is just will protest that the laws must be modified, leaving them usually with the task of providing an alternative rationale for whatever they endeavour to put in place of the status quo.

So what underpins any legal system is generally some claim that it delivers justice and order. For any such system to be justified it needs to be securely anchored on agreed moral principles: but they are in short supply. While some sense of the need for order is to be found in any human society, the ideas that are entertained about justice and order itself differ profoundly. Where, the recurrent problem is, are the commonalities there? Does not cultural relativity reign supreme in matters of right and wrong?

Attempts to find valid robust cross-cultural universals in the domain of morality have often failed to deliver (cf. Hauser 2006). Perhaps the most promising candidate is some notion of what has been called the Golden Rule. This comes in a negative version—do not do to others what you would not have them do to you—and also a positive one: behave towards others as you would have them behave towards you. Some such principle has been found in or attributed to otherwise quite divergent teachers and teachings, Confucius, Socrates, the Old Testament, Zoroaster, and some Buddhist texts. Yet on other issues they have very different lessons to convey and they can hardly be said to have advocated one and the same set of ethical provisions. Confucius is interpreted as placing the emphasis on social relations. Each individual should behave to others according to the norms proper to their particular position, the father should be fatherly, the son filial, elder brothers and younger ones should behave towards one another in the appropriate ways, and so on. Socrates argued that the way ahead starts with self-knowledge, often, he thought, in short supply in the society in which he lived. Buddhist texts take their starting-point in an acceptance that the phenomenal world is mere illusion, while Zoroastrian ones see that world as a battle between Good and Evil. The Old Testament insists on the exceptionality of the Chosen People, a doctrine that is transformed, in Christianity, into one of a contrast between the Saved and the Damned. Christ comes to save the sins of all humans, but those who were born too early to have knowledge of His Redemption or were otherwise ignorant of His Mission suffer from a certain handicap that Christians found, and still find, hard to explain satisfactorily.

Over and over again high-level theological or metaphysical disputes have cast a long shadow over the nature of the provision for justice that is attempted by any given society. When the focus is on attaining perman-ent bliss in Heaven or at least in avoiding perpetual damnation in Hell, justice in behaviour to one's fellows may occupy only an inferior role in the scale of values to be cultivated. The emphasis may be rather on the purity of one's soul, even just the correct performance of the appropriate rituals (felicity again). God's judgement, it is assumed, will be a just one: all of us will get our just deserts. But obedience to authority may figure more prominently than how well one has lived up to the ideals of some moral principle such as a Golden Rule, let alone to more detailed provisions such as are set out in the Ten Commandments.

None of this should be supposed to detract from the universality of the claims I put forward in Chapter 5, concerning the basic social character of humans despite our all living in very different polities. But the mere fact of human sociability by itself yields little by way of positive conclu-sions on which to base claims for fundamental commonalities in moral-ity and correspondingly little on the further issue of the concept of justice that should underpin legality. Some version of the Golden Rule, we said, is probably the best candidate. But faced with dogmatic intolerance, it is altogether too idealistic to expect that a policy of turning the other cheek will persuade the intolerant to mend their ways. We must rely on force or the threat of it to deliver security (Runciman 2009), though that is not to say that we can be satisfied that the laws we currently live under require no revision. On the contrary, any inadequacy in those legal provisions is likely to fuel aggressive reactions in what in most cases will turn into a vicious circle. Biased laws or unfair implementation will lead to dissidents taking the law, as we say, into their own hands, where the usual answer from the authorities will be forcible repression all too likely to lead to more sense of unfairness.

The problems are aggravated when one or other of two common conditions is fulfilled, when either the perceived opportunities for revising the existing laws are minimal or when those responsible for applying them constitute a closed elite that has nothing but their own interests at heart. Aristotle, once again, identifies the first problem when he drew attention to the fact that any change to the existing *nomoi* (covering both law and custom or convention) is liable to weaken the authority of the legal system as a whole (*Politics* 1269a19–24, cf. Brunschwig 1980).[2] He accordingly thought that extreme caution should be exercised when such revision is proposed. However, on one issue, namely on who was in a position to influence any such revision, the democratic regimes with which he was familiar—although he disapproved of them—ensured that a far wider constituency had a chance to have its views heard than most other ancient regimes permitted. Even so, to be sure, even the most radical ancient Greek democracies still excluded women and slaves.

Greek democracies were also in a better position than most to avoid the major problems I mentioned under the second head. The police force, if one can call it such, consisted of slaves, under the control of magistrates. But both those magistrates and other officials in positions of executive responsibility were subject to scrutiny at the end of their terms of office and most of the important posts were anything but permanent. The most powerful officers of state, the generals, were elected for a year and though in some famous cases, such as Pericles, they were re-elected a number of times, that always depended on the continuing approval of the citizen body as a whole. The Athenians also invented a particular device, that of ostracism, that could be used to remove powerful individuals for a period from the city, and proposals to hold an ostracism in any given year could be on the initiative of any citizen. We have concrete epigraphic evidence that ostracisms

---

[2] Similarly, in ancient China, both the *Shangjunshu* (1.1.26–2.2) and the *Lüshi Chunqiu* (15.8) record debates on the question of the circumstances in which the laws can be changed (Lloyd 2009: 118–19).

sometimes occurred, though only during a limited period in the exist-ence of the democracy (Vanderpool 1970).

None of this can take us very far in support of any claim we might like to make that a sense of the need for justice, let alone the sense of a need for a particular construal of what justice is, can be said to be a human universal. Child psychologists have indeed adduced good evidence that a sense of fair play is common already in very young infants.[3] However, the enormous variety of concepts and practices of justice that history and anthropology reveal suggests that that basic sense of fairness comes to be overlaid by layers of complex responses to the actual social and political arrangements that they face as adult members of the society to which they belong. A concern for self-interest will often trump many more altruistic motivations, even though some sense of fairness may remain deep down. Ancient societies as well as modern ones have struggled to find adequate solutions to problems of governance, and there seems to be an inverse correlation between the ability of a regime to secure stability and its fostering, or at least not strangling, the opportunities of individ-uals or groups to suggest that things might be improved.

Further one may note that while some evolutionary and cross-cultural studies (e.g. Curry et al. 2019) suggest that a capacity for fairness and cooperation is built into our social essence, others have pointed rather in a different direction. According to this latter view, as we have noted before, what we have inherited from our ancestors is an instinct for aggressive behaviour. We are certainly not the only higher primates who engage in the slaughter of our conspecifics, for that has been observed most dramatically in chimpanzees (Goodall 1986; the story of the effect of this discovery on the debate about human nature in the USA has been told by Milam 2018). In one version of a social Darwinian argument the survival of the fittest depends not just on their protecting themselves but on removing, that is probably exterminating, all rivals, conspecifics, or close relatives included. That, it is supposed, may well have happened in the course of the extinction of Neanderthals with the rise of modern humans. Thus such instinctive aggression has as good a chance of being a universal human trait as any nascent sense of justice—where of course

---

[3] A similar point is made by the philosopher Gary Matthews on the basis of his work with school-children: Matthews 1984, 1994.

both those twin intuitions can to some extent be salvaged with the argument that it is the in-group to which one owes an obligation of fairness while outsiders merit no such accommodation. Yet the effect of any such argument is, to be sure, to limit the scope of application of the Golden Rule severely.

At this final point a new vulnerability of law emerges. While it covers all those accepted as one's fellows in whatever society one belongs to, those who belong to other groups are excluded, and conversely the members of other communities accept no obligation to live by anyone else's laws and customs but their own. Some Greeks discussed this problem under the rubric of unwritten laws, supposed to be valid across all humans.[4] But the difficulty that their debates revealed was that of identifying what those non-society-specific laws comprised. Incest was one favoured candidate, until it was realized that that was breached in such societies as Egypt. That implicitly raised the question of what exactly is to count as incest, but it served nevertheless to undermine claims that it was an unproblematic universal taboo. Loving one's parents was another common proposal in the Old Testament as well as in both Greece and China. Yet that was a principle that was breached even more frequently.

Awareness of human diversity in the matter of customs, in notions of legality and of morality has today increased beyond measure compared with ancient societies. But attempts to settle on a workable and fair system of international law show no signs of reaching a successful conclusion. True, we have institutions such as the International Court of Justice and the International Criminal Court whose task it is to secure justice and punish war crimes across international boundaries. But aside from the bureaucratic cumbersomeness with which those institutions function, and the political interference to which they may be subject, their claims for legitimacy are not as robust, nor as universally agreed, as

[4] Versions of this appear in Sophocles *Antigone* 453ff., Herodotus 7. 136 (where the speaker is Xerxes, no less), in Thucydides 2. 37.3 (Pericles commenting on how the Athenians observe such unwritten laws), and in Xenophon's *Memorabilia* 4.4.18ff., where Hippias and Socrates disagree on what the unwritten laws include. The ideal of trying to base legal provisions on universal moral principles was the driving force behind many later theories, such as the *ius gentium* or *ius naturale* of the Roman jurists, or of the notion of 'natural law' advocated by Grotius, among many others. Yet any such ambition always confronted the difficulty of establishing any such principles in the first place.

one would wish. They may offer our best hope for the future. But their present performance illustrates the twin difficulties I have been exploring in this chapter, that of identifying reliable universal moral principles and then that of devising the institutions to convert those into a viable legal system.

That certainly does not mean that we are reduced to concluding that there is nothing to choose between one view of right and wrong and any other. But we have to acknowledge that claims for universal moral principles do not generally extend to cover the types of detailed problems that are the essence of legal systems. Those systems achieve greater or less success in securing order, but the shortfall in the regime of justice they aim to ensure arises not only from the frailties of human interpreters endeavouring to apply principles to particular cases, but also from the conceptual difficulty of saying just what justice is. There is enough evidence to ground the claim that as the social animals we are, we have an inbuilt sense of fairness to our fellows as a positive value. But all too often, as we noted, the expression of any such idealistic sentiment is thwarted by narrow considerations of the interest of groups or of individuals within them, which are generally fuelled by far more powerful instincts.

So to be realistic, we are faced with some sobering conclusions. The viability of law as a cross-cultural category is threatened first by the fact that many societies have no codified system and make do with inevitably looser norms governing how people should behave and to which they should be committed. Where explicit legal provisions exist to be implemented, the converse difficulties relate to their adequacy, in principle or in practice, to secure fairness not just for a small elite, but for the community as a whole, including in its relations to other communities. When individuals or groups sense any such shortfall, existing laws become, for them, an impediment, not a means, to justice, though if they are to be replaced the recurrent issue is how to do any better. For sure, it is not that the quests for better legal arrangements and less imperfect implementation of them are futile. But the thinness, if not also the disputability, of any agreed moral basis for justice must always jeopardize the bid to secure its provision.

11

Test Case 4: Aesthetics

Art and Music

Aesthetics is in all likelihood the most problematic of all the categories I am here examining in these studies of human universals and cross-cultural relativities. I shall divide my discussion into three parts. The first will deal very briefly with what we call the plastic arts, such as painting, sculpture, and architecture, where I shall explore the applicability of our Western concepts and suggest the relevance of the contrast between felicity and efficacy that I have introduced in Chapter 3. I turn next to the rather different area of music, where there are some sophisticated extant analyses both of harmonies and of the values they may express from our ancient sources, which can help us to appreciate something of the diversity of musical experience and reflections on that across the world. The final part of the chapter is devoted to an examination of the most systematic attempt at a taxonomy correlating artistic styles with ontologies, namely that of Descola (2010) which raises in the sharpest terms the question of whether we are dealing with a single coherent category, of the aesthetic, across human experience. Evidently ideas about what is beautiful differ widely, but is 'beauty' a concept that can sensibly be applied across cultures?

We may assume that we can recognize beautiful art objects wherever or whenever in the world they have been produced. But that will often depend on our using, indeed imposing, our actors' categories, where those who produced those objects may have had very different ones and possibly no distinct explicit concept corresponding to 'art' as such at all. This was a point that Edmund Leach made much of in his discussion in 1954. Obviously not just any object that we count as beautiful will also count as 'art', only those where there has been some human intervention

Intelligence and Intelligibility: Cross-Cultural Studies of Human Cognitive Experience. G. E. R. Lloyd, Oxford University Press (2020). © G. E. R. Lloyd.
DOI: 10.1093/oso/9780198854593.001.0001

in the production or at the least the adaptation of the object in question. But that inevitably implicates the intentionality of the humans concerned and so raises questions about how far their actors' categories match our observers' ones. In cases where they seem to fail to match even approximately, we face a dilemma. If we say that we have no option but to use our criteria, that may be thought to undermine any claim that aesthetic experience is universal. If we allow actors' categories to guide us, that still leaves the problem of accounting for the mismatch.

Any confidence that easy answers are to be found will be dented not just by confronting the ethnographic data but also by delving into our own recent and not so recent history, where 'our' covers modern European societies where some notion of 'art' exists.[1] Particularly dramatic changes in taste occurred in the last century. The traditional view of art as basically representational has been not just challenged but effectively overthrown, with the extreme wing of the revolutionaries prepared to claim that anything can be said to be art if anyone decides to call it so. The battle then becomes one not about the dividing line between good art and bad, but on what comes within the scope of the category of art at all,[2] and the questions are no mere matters of understanding and definition, but issues with considerable commercial implications. Nor is this just a modern European phenomenon. We find examples of arbiters of taste in sixteenth- and seventeenth-century China promoting particular artistic styles in which they themselves had invested heavily where what was at stake was not just a matter of aesthetics but of financial gain (Clunas 1991, 1997).

The understanding of the ethnographic data was transformed particularly by Gell (1998) in a pioneering work that drew attention to the ways in which what we might suppose to be just artistic creations were imagined very differently by the actors concerned. Where a Western observer might not look past the beautiful craftsmanship of a wooden prow board for a canoe, that, Gell showed (and cf. Scoditti 1990), is

---

[1] We sometimes use the term 'art' where neither the activity nor the end-product has any pretensions to meet some criterion of what is aesthetically attractive (as when we speak of the 'art' of war, for instance, where we are referring to the skills involved). Here, I am concerned rather with activities and objects where some such aim or ambition is in play.

[2] Compare the distinction we drew in Chapter 9 between saying that other religions are false and saying that they are not religion at all.

drastically to underestimate and to misconstrue what the craftsmen themselves are trying to achieve and how their work will be appreciated. Sculptures, weaving, body-painting may all be primarily concerned not with beauty but with power and agency. To use the contrast we have introduced before, the goal is not, or not just, felicity, but efficacy, in this case the production of an effect which may be compared with what linguists call the 'perlocutionary' force of a statement, that is, how it affects the audience to which it is addressed. In the case of what we may think of superficially as 'art' objects, immense efforts may be put into producing objects that will have the effect of positively intimidating those who see them. Of course magnificence in monumental architecture and sculpture has often been a goal of Western art as well. But Gell's point is rather that such an effect may be sought after to the point of eclipsing what an observer would class as the aesthetic qualities of the object concerned.

In many instances, the objects that now figure in our museums and art galleries have no accompanying commentary from the native craftsmen who made them that will help us to gain access to their ideas about their work. But sometimes we have some detailed evidence on the question, as in such ethnographic reports as those of Scoditti who spent many months learning wood-carving on the island of Kitawa. His account (Scoditti 1990) includes detailed verbatim records of conversations that he had with teachers and others who made it clear that skill as a wood-carver depended certainly on possessing a rare natural talent but then also on long apprenticeship with an acknowledged master. He also points out that in their society, as in ours, skill in judging the quality of the end-product was not shared equally across the community, for the craftsmen themselves were looked up to as special connoisseurs in the domain.

But most importantly the end result of their work was to be judged not so much by the pleasure it gave, as by how successful it was in producing the desired effect of amazing those who saw it. This was a community that engaged extensively in travel and trade with others on islands at varying distances from Kitawa in what is known as the Kula ring. Their canoes were built not just for utilitarian purposes, but to impress. When a canoe with a particularly striking prow board arrived at a neighbouring island, the expected result was not just that the islanders should take some delight in seeing such a wonderful object. It was assumed that their being so impressed would have a direct impact on the terms of trade with which business, that is exchange, would be conducted. The canoes played an important part in securing the commercial success of the visit and so also of the political standing of the visitors.

This and other evidence goes to show that our usual notions of aesthetics are not directly translatable into those of other peoples, ancient or modern. Yet of course that does not mean that we remain at a total loss to understand anything of their experience. Notions of what is beautiful may be entangled with others that relate to the efficacy of the objects concerned, as well as to their felicity or appropriateness, including, for example, their suitability as objects of worship. While that means that if we expect to find an equivalent to a category of 'pure' aesthetic experience in every human society we shall be disappointed, it should not lead us to conclude that we can understand simply nothing of how the objects are made, of the intentions of their makers, and of how and why, on what grounds, they are appreciated, though all of that involves harder work than we might initially have supposed. What counts as 'beautiful' varies from group to group, as does whether some notion of 'beauty' is the effect that is sought and by which objects will be evaluated. However, a recognition of the power to impress that some objects possess is also, and sometimes more widely, attested, even while that still leaves plenty of variation in how that impressiveness is judged. Besides, appreciating intentions is, for sure, far from the only element involved in any effort to 'understand' a work of art, where we usually recognize that our current understanding can be extended and improved.

Now let me turn to the rather different circumstances of an appreciation of music. Faced with the quite amazing variety of musical experiences described and indeed recorded from across the world, produced by so many different types of wind, string, and percussion instruments and by voice, ethnomusicologists have struggled to identify cross-cultural commonalities (Blacking 1987).[3] It is true that the concords of octave, fifth, and fourth (as we label them) are widely recognized as harmonious, and their correlation with the ratios 1:2, 2:3, and 3:4 is also attested in

---

[3] Thus recent studies by Mehr and colleagues (Mehr et al. 2018) based on a wide variety of data serve to confirm and elaborate the suggestion advanced some time ago by Trehub, Unyk, and Trainor (1993) to the effect that adults are able to distinguish music that is directed towards infants, as opposed to adults, across cultures.

different cultures, including both ancient Greece and ancient China. Yet that provides us with only a minimal starting-point for any account of musical appreciation. Beyond the recognition of those basic concords, those Greek and Chinese analyses of musical phenomena diverged sharply. The highly complex Greek classification of the various modes involved intervals such as the so-called *leimma*, represented by the ratio of 256 to 243 (Barker 1989) and the Chinese developed an equivalent to the twelve-tone scale (for example in the second-century BCE compilation *Huainanzi* ch. 3: 21b).

The question that much of our evidence poses is whether musicality as such (whatever we mean by that) is the appropriate analytic category. Very often, and indeed in both those ancient societies we have mentioned, the quality of the sounds is no purely aesthetic matter (as we might say) but rather one of morality. Confucius, famously, was overwhelmed by the delights of the music of certain regions but condemned that of others as licentious (*Lunyu* 7.14, 15.11). In Greece some modes were agreed to promote courage and virtue, others debauchery.

It is often the case, too, that music has a crucial role to play in ritual and in religious experience, which further complicates our understanding of the actors' categories in question. Hugh-Jones' study of the use of music among the Barasana in NW Amazonia is exemplary. They have both trumpets and percussion instruments as well as flutes. The latter, the so-called Yurupari flutes, are particularly important. One story of their origin has it that they were stolen by women. But in present-day society they are played only by men. While women must hear the sound of the flutes, they are not permitted to see them (Hugh-Jones 2017).[4] The power of the music depends not just on the quality of the sound but on the ritual propriety of the performance, the purity of the performers and the correct behaviour of their audiences. But while analogous circumstances may surround music-playing in other societies, the specific rules that obtain among the Barasana are theirs alone.

Once again then cross-cultural divergences figure more prominently in our analysis than the commonalities we can identify. What we may call aesthetic considerations carry important moral and religious

---

[4] That is the rule that is laid down: but in practice women do often break it and see as well as hear the flutes being played.

associations, to the point where it may be more correct to say not that the aesthetic domain contributes to morality, but rather than the aesthetic domain as such does not figure as an independent actors' category. As we have found in other studies, our starting assumptions about the analytic map of human experience that we bring to bear have to be adjusted to begin to do justice to the variety we find.

However, we have yet to consider the biggest challenge to the cross-cultural comparability of the category of the aesthetic. This is posed by the correlation between artistic styles and ontologies themselves proposed by Descola and his colleagues. Descola (2013) put forward an ambitious taxonomy of the divergent ontologies to be found across the world. These were distinguished by the assumptions made first on physicality (the stuff things are made of) and second, on interiority (notions of self-hood, the mind, the soul). The taxonomy then proceeds by way of a contrast, in each case, between a view that stresses continuity and one that emphasizes discontinuity.

This double differentiation yields a four-fold schema, for which he uses the labels 'animism', 'totemism', 'analogism', and 'naturalism', though the first two terms are radically redefined from their usage by Tylor, for example, or by Lévi-Strauss (1969). 'Animism' stresses continuity on the interiority axis (other creatures besides humans have spirits) but discontinuity on the physicality one (different beings are differentiated by the different bodies they possess). 'Totemism', next, assumes continuity in both physicality and interiority. 'Analogism' conversely presupposes discontinuity on both axes. Finally 'naturalism', the default position of Western modernity, assumes discontinuity between humans and other creatures on the interiority axis, but continuity on the physicality one: everything is made of the same stuff.

These proposals have generated an enormous literature in anthropology and were a major contributor, along with the equally influential work of Viveiros de Castro (1998, 2014), to the flurry of studies associated with what is called the 'ontological turn'.[5] In the process several aspects of Descola's schema have been challenged, notably the extent to which these ontologies are self-contained and mutually exclusive systems, and

---

[5] Cf. Chapter 6, p. 52.

the robustness of the category of 'analogistic' regimes in particular.[6] Thus Viveiros de Castro, for instance, agrees in seeing a basic contrast between the 'naturalism' of modernity and what Descola called 'animism', though Viveiros prefers to operate with the wider category of what he calls 'perspectivism'. The key contrast is between a view that presupposes that nature is universal, while cultures differ, on the one hand, and the reverse position that has it that culture is universal and natures differ, that is between the mononaturalism plus multiculturalism of Western modernity and indigenous multinaturalism and monoculturalism.[7]

The relevance of these debates for my present purposes here lies in the further developments that occurred when Descola proposed correlating artistic styles with his four ontologies. Descola (2010) provides a running commentary on a remarkable exhibition at the Musée du Quai Branly in Paris that gathered together an inspiring collection of art objects (as we would call them) from across the world, arranging them, precisely, to illustrate the differences between 'animism' 'totemism' 'analogism', and 'naturalism'. Thus indigenous Australian paintings are indeed full of images that manifest the assumptions of 'totemism' as do the wood carvings from British Columbia. Again 'naturalism', associated here with a notion of 'objectivity', is not hard to exemplify with Western art since the Renaissance.

Yet of course there are points at which this taxonomy as applied to art can be challenged. While Descola sees 'analogism' as the dominant regime throughout Greco-Roman antiquity, late Hellenistic and Roman portraiture has more in common with 'naturalism' than he perhaps allowed, and the same might be said of Pompeian landscapes and even Minoan depictions of flora and fauna. As others have noted (and cf. n. 6), the four-fold schema as originally proposed finds it difficult to deal satisfactorily with hybrids, even though Descola himself was very well aware of how prevalent they are.

---

[6] The four-fold taxonomy was certainly presented in Descola (2013) as if the four in question were to be distinguished by mutually incompatible assumptions about physicality and interiority, but in practice overlaps between them were recognized in the ethnographic record. I have argued that the differences between ancient Greece and China make it difficult to see both as examples of 'analogistic' regimes (e.g. Lloyd 2007: 144).

[7] As Latour (2009) pointed out, for Viveiros de Castro what is at stake is not so much a typology of ontologies as an argument between opposing political agenda.

But none of these problems is as important as the question raised by the potential implications of this classification for what we mean by 'art' in the first place. The difficulty may be expressed like this. If what we superficially think of as 'art' objects represent radically different perspectives on the world, which some would see as different worlds, indeed, how is it possible to discuss and compare them without drastically distorting their original function for the actors who created and used them? We have seen how the anthropology of music shows how it may convey very different values. But since we are familiar enough with the cultural differences in value systems, this does not threaten our assumption that at one level at least we are dealing with a single category, that of the experience of musicality. Insofar as we accept Descola's suggestion that what we label 'art' may reflect divergent and incompatible regimes of ontology, the prospect looms that we are dealing with experiences that it would be quite mistaken to lump together under any single such rubric. However, that may go against the grain of his project in one cardinal respect. By bringing his objects together and comparing them, that implicitly presupposes that they have something in common even while they exhibit profoundly divergent ontological views. On that story we have to learn that our usual Western critiques may be well wide of the mark, but may still keep a revised notion of 'art' in play rather than vetoing its use as hopelessly misleading.

It is time to take stock. Concessions surely must be made that our category of 'art', insofar as that continues to reflect a general assumption that we are dealing just with what has a claim to be beautiful by some criterion, is seriously inadequate when we attempt to apply it cross-culturally. The objects to which we attach that label often serve functions analogous to the perlocutionary force of speech acts—designed to produce an effect on their audience. The ways in which such effects may be generated certainly reflect how the group in question sees itself in relation to other beings, to the environment and to the world in which they live, as well as the fundamental values it holds dear. Indeed the objects that we may categorize as 'art' may provide precious insight into just such issues.

Thus far we can agree that there are radical differences in the ontological presuppositions in the different objects made and used by different peoples across the world and this has profound repercussions for our understanding of their roles. If we apply our notions, including on such matters as the criteria to judge 'representation', and even on the character of the contrast between nature and culture themselves, we are liable to misinterpret how these objects are appreciated in their original contexts and fail to grasp the aims of the craftsmen who made them.

To be sure, that does not mean that all understanding is irrevocably beyond our reach. To make some progress we should make the best use we can of the actors' own reports on their endeavours as well as the anthropologists' commentaries on those. But the price we have to pay is to have to acknowledge that many of our initial assumptions have drastically to be overhauled if we are to do justice to the variety of the phenomena in the ethnographic and historical records. The category of 'art', to be fit for purpose, needs to be revised in order to allow for the goal of efficacy as well as that of felicity. The domain of the 'aesthetic' is not hermetically sealed off from that of morality. It is as difficult to lay down what peoples in different groups consider to be aesthetically pleasing as it is to specify what they take pleasure in on any grounds. We should not retreat to the weak-kneed dictum that 'beauty' is 'in the eye of the beholder' as if that were an arbitrary matter, for it is anything but that when it serves as a basic social value. Above all, we need to recognize the still limited and parochial nature of our current Western notions of the experience of art, even after the revolutions in those notions that have taken place in the last century and a half.

My last chapter will endeavour to summarize our findings in our attempts to do justice to the twin initial intuitions, of cross-cultural human commonalities, and evident cultural diversity, and to offer a final commentary on the fundamental issue of mutual intelligibility.

Conclusion

Towards More Ecumenical Analyses

As our wide-ranging explorations have shown, intelligence takes so many different forms that any attempt to propose a single definitive account of all its manifestations must be considered foolhardy. We recognize it not just in humans but in other animals, and not just in living beings, but also in inanimate ones, as when we speak of the artificial intelligence of computers. Sometimes we assess it by the speed or efficiency or reliability shown in drawing inferences from data, though those three criteria may yield conflicting judgements, as when speed may be bought at the price of reliability. But sometimes intelligence is not a matter of self-conscious reasoning, nor one of extracting conclusions from data, but is shown in behaviour, in practical activity, in perform-ance, in dexterity, in understanding others in the sense of sympathizing with them. Then it may not be mediated through language but rather embodied.

Where human intelligence is concerned, the chief focus of our interest here, the problem we identified at the outset was that of reconciling two opposing intuitions. On the one hand, as the human beings we all are, we may have a strong sense of the basic cognitive capacities we all share. On the other hand, we are just as acutely aware of where we differ, from members of our own society, and even more so from others, in our patterns of behaviour, practices, skills, values, and understandings. When we focus on the commonalities we may be lulled into a sense that there is no need to investigate further and probe beneath the surface to find where there may be possible divergences. Conversely, when we encounter striking cultural differences, an extreme reaction is to give up and conclude that each culture, maybe even each group within it, can

Intelligence and Intelligibility: Cross-Cultural Studies of Human Cognitive Experience. G. E. R. Lloyd, Oxford University Press (2020). © G. E. R. Lloyd.
DOI: 10.1093/oso/9780198854593.001.0001

only be understood 'from within', that is by the members of the community concerned.

In each of our studies we have found ample evidence for my two initial opposing intuitions. All humans possess language, and while the differences between different natural languages pose severe problems of translation, these can to some extent be overcome, even if at the cost of patient and laborious commentary and paraphrase. In any event we have to recognize that perfect understanding of any given speech act is impossible, not just across languages, but within a single one. Yet as I have repeatedly emphasized, realization of the unattainability of complete comprehension should not lead us to forget how much we can provisionally understand in one another's mundane activities and communications.

Again, all humans live in some society. Even though societies exemplify many different types of organization, have different interests and values, and cultivate different practices, that does not undermine the point that we are all social animals.

Thus far a modest claim for human universals can be sustained. But when we examine different areas of cognitive activity, we find that different analyses are applicable in different instances. Our investigations underline the importance of not ignoring two types of lesson, one concerning the tools of analysis we use, the other to do with the categories of cognitive experiences themselves. Under the first head I pointed to the ways in which our familiar dichotomies of the literal and the metaphorical, and of magic and rational account, may mislead. First of all, these are more often our observers' categories than actors' ones, when the peoples we study draw no such distinctions explicitly or even implicitly. Second, those binaries may and often do distort our interpretations of the communicative exchanges in question. We need, rather, to recover the original actors' ways of discriminating between different modes of discourse, paying attention, for example, to the different degrees of seriousness with which exchanges are conducted and to the pragmatics of those situations. That cannot, to be sure, be thought to resolve all the puzzlements of interpretation we face. But it may serve to make us hesitate before diagnosing stark irrationality and sheer folly in others, or at least doing so very much more readily than when we are dealing with members of our own society.

Then second, so far as the categories of cognitive experience we examined go, I suggested that the appropriate response is not the same in all the test cases I chose for discussion. In some, at least, the differences we encounter relate not so much to different cognitive capacities, as to the applicability of our own common assumptions. Where mathematics is concerned, an argument can be mounted that every society has some appreciation and use for quantity, number, shapes, and forms, even though how that works out in practice differs considerably. But religion poses a different problem, where there are graver difficulties in identifying what counts as such in the first place, and plenty of societies that do not have beliefs or practices that qualify on several of the preferred criteria. Again while some ways of maintaining order exist in every society, calling all of these legal systems may carry positive overtones inappropriate to the informality of some of them. Finally when we came to discuss aesthetics we again found that reservations and modifications need to be made to our concepts for them to apply to the varied experiences that are attested round the world and across time. In this context especially, some of our own notions about art seem unhelpful when we try to apply them cross-culturally.

That last point encapsulates one of the general lessons we can take away from our surveys, the need to recognize the different degrees of viability of many of our common assumptions about human experience when we consider the issues globally. It is true that in the past many commentators, faced with the more striking differences that we find in modes of thought, adopted a very different tactic. Western modernity, they maintained, provides the models by which other regimes are to be judged, and mostly to be found wanting. We have the right answers to the questions, the right methods to yield solutions. Yet such intellectual imperialism faces obstacles that vary from the moderate to the most severe. We cannot conceivably claim that the English language, or some European one, is the only one fit for fruitful communication, despite the numerous claims that have been made to some such effect. The shortcomings in our political systems on both a national and an international scale have become all too obvious in the last hundred years. The disastrous consequences that generally follow when any group claims they adhere to the one true religion are there for all to see, even though some individuals and groups are still in denial on the subject. Similarly we cannot say we have a monopoly of the only worthwhile or correct notions in the domain of aesthetics, either about that domain itself or on the products our connoisseurs are in business evaluating.

It is particularly where science and the scientific method are concerned that Western hegemonic assumptions seem plausible to many. But even here, perhaps especially here, we should hesitate, or so I have argued, on three main grounds. First the total coherence of what we tend for pedagogical purposes to represent as *the* scientific method is open to question, as also, second, is whether or how far 'it' actually corresponds to the practice of scientists in every domain, indeed in some instances in any. Third, science should not be judged by results (for they are always revisable) but by certain aims and practices, observation, classification, explanation, prediction, testing in trial and error procedures if not in fully explicit experimentation. The advances that have been made in cosmology, physics, biology do indeed allow us to claim that we know and understand more about many topics than our predecessors, though many of the contested problems we are interested in were simply not on their agenda. Conversely most of us who live in highly urbanized environments have lost much of the know-how exhibited in indigenous communities including especially about plants and animals (cf. Atran, Medin, and Ross 2004). Moreover even adopting our ideas of science as a yardstick, there is so much more for us to learn. As we have put it before, the recognition of the extent of what is still beyond our reach grows as quickly as, sometimes more quickly than, our grasp of the problems that we have succeeded in resolving satisfactorily, at least so far as our present, provisional, understanding goes.

But if thus far I have argued that the basic commonalities across the human race are not substantially threatened by our vivid sense of the differences that also exist among us, I must return to the deeper manifestations of the difficulties of mutual understanding. I certainly cannot and would not deny that communication often breaks down, not just when different languages or conceptual frameworks confront one another, but also especially when different value systems do so. While I would still maintain that some mutual comprehension is always, in principle, possible, it may well not be achieved in practice, not just when there is no desire to understand others, even a refusal to concede that they are worth understanding, but also where the assumptions brought to the task have not been subjected to proper critical scrutiny such as I have been attempting here. It is ironic that one of the most striking examples of this comes from the early history of attempts to overcome the difficulties by engaging in serious anthropological study. It seemed obvious not just to Frazer, but also to the far more perceptively analytic Lévy-Bruhl, that primitive peoples suffered from radical cognitive deficiencies—and some such assumption lingered on even in those who had extensive field work experience, such as Malinowski and Evans-Pritchard. That was sometimes rather to turn a blind eye to the multiple manifestations of folly shown by the members of even the most 'advanced' societies and we must add that includes folly in attributing folly to others.

I must, in conclusion, repeat the caveats I expressed at the outset. My own forays into these deep issues suffer from the limitations in my own expertise that I noted. My own reflections stem in the first instance from my inquiry into ancient societies and while their exceptionality should not be exaggerated, they can evidently not be held up as typical representatives of the human experience. But if they cannot be used as reliable bases for any attempt to arrive at general solutions to our problems, they certainly provide good evidence for their complexity. In the final analysis I come away from those and my other readings in ethnography with a clear sense, on the one hand, of where certain mistakes have been made and on the other, of how by making the most of the kind of test cases I have considered we can derive some hope for future understandings.

It is by juxtaposing very different human experiences that we can discover the limitations of any given perspective. The recognition of striking differences is, as I have put it, an opportunity, not a threat, let alone a sign that we humans are all stuck in a morass of inevitable mutual misunderstanding. Already anthropological and historical studies such as I have undertaken suggest how they can serve as models for the revisability that I advocate, and that includes revision of our initial assumptions even on the most fundamental issues, those that lie at the heart of our conceptual framework and are basic to our habitual methodology. These include the notion of nature itself and what is taken as its antonym, namely 'culture', as well as those of person, causation, and agency, and again the concepts of the metaphorical, of myth, and of rationality itself. There is no doubt a great deal more that is there to be learnt not just by extending those investigations but also by joining forces with those pursuing other avenues of research in areas of experimental psychology and cognitive science which I am not qualified to tackle. Nevertheless my hope is that the conceptual clarifications I have proposed will prove relevant and useful for others embarking on other cross-disciplinary and cross-cultural inquiries. The task of achieving a better understanding of one another should surely elicit our most strenuous efforts. No one could be more aware than I am of the difficulties of that task. But I yield to none in a sense of its importance.

Bibliography

This gives details of all the books and articles to which I refer, together with a brief selection of other texts that discuss related problems and have influenced my thinking.

Acemoglu, D. and Robinson, J.A. (2012) *Why Nations Fail: The Origins of Power, Prosperity and Poverty* (New York).

Aikhenvald, A.Y. (2004) *Evidentiality* (Oxford).

Ascher, M. (1991) *Ethnomathematics: A Multicultural View of Mathematical Ideas* (Pacific Grove).

Atran, S. (1990) *Cognitive Foundations of Natural History* (Cambridge).

Atran, S. (1998) 'Folk Biology and the Anthropology of Science. Cognitive Universals and Cultural Particulars', *Behavioral and Brain Sciences* 21: 547–609.

Atran, S. (2002) *In Gods We Trust: The Evolutionary Landscape of Religion* (Oxford).

Atran, S. (2010) *Talking to the Enemy: Faith, Brotherhood, and the (Un)making of Terrorists* (New York).

Atran, S., Medin, D., and Ross, N. (2004) 'Evolution and Devolution of Knowledge: A Tale of Two Biologies', *Journal of the Royal Anthropological Institute* 10: 395–420.

Austin, J.L. (1962) *How to Do Things with Words* (Oxford).

Avital, E. and Jablonka, E. (2000) *Animal Traditions: Behavioural Inheritance in Evolution* (Cambridge).

Barker, A. (1989) *Greek Musical Writings II: Harmonic and Acoustic Theory* (Cambridge).

Barkow, J.H., Cosmides, L., and Tooby, J. (eds) (1992) *The Adapted Mind: Evolutionary Psychology and the Generation of Culture* (Oxford).

Barnes, J. (1991) 'Galen on Logic and Therapy', in R.J. Durling and F. Kudlien (eds) *Galen's Method of Healing* (Leiden) pp. 50–102.

Barnes, S. Barry (1973) 'The Comparison of Belief-Systems: Anomaly versus Falsehood', in Horton and Finnegan (1973) pp. 182–98.

Barnes, S. Barry (1974) *Scientific Knowledge and Sociological Theory* (London).

Barnes, S. Barry and Bloor, D. (1982) 'Relativism, Rationalism and the Sociology of Knowledge', in Hollis and Lukes (1982) pp. 21–47.

Baron-Cohen, S. (2003) *The Essential Difference: Men, Women and the Extreme Male Brain* (London).

Baron-Cohen, S. and Harrison, J.E. (1997) *Synaesthesia* (Oxford).

Barrett, J.L. (2000) 'Exploring the Natural Foundations of Religion', *Trends in Cognitive Sciences* 4.1: 29–34.

Barrett, J.L. and Keil, F.C. (1996) 'Conceptualizing a Nonnatural Entity: Anthropomorphism in God Concepts', *Cognitive Psychology* 31.3: 219–47.

Barth, F. (1975) *Ritual and Knowledge among the Baktaman of New Guinea* (Oslo).

Bateson, P. and Gluckman, P. (2011) *Plasticity, Robustness, Development and Evolution* (Cambridge).

Baumard, N. and Boyer, P. (2013) 'Explaining Moral Religions', *Trends in Cognitive Sciences* 17.6: 272–80.

Baumard, N., Hyafil, A., Morris, I., and Boyer, P. (2015) 'Increased Affluence Explains the Emergence of Ascetic Wisdoms and Moralizing Religions', *Current Biology* 25.1: 10–15.

Baylor, D. (1995) 'Colour Mechanisms of the Eye', in T. Lamb and J. Bourriau (eds) *Colour: Art and Science* (Cambridge) pp. 103–26.

Bellah, R.N. (2005) 'What is Axial about the Axial Age?' *Archives Européennes de Sociologie* 46: 69–89.

Bellah, R.N. (2011) *Religion in Human Evolution* (Cambridge, MA).

Berlin, B. and Kay, P. (1969) *Basic Color Terms: Their Universality and Evolution* (Berkeley, CA).

Berryman, S. (2009) *The Mechanical Hypothesis in Ancient Greek Natural Philosophy* (Cambridge).

Billig, M. (1991) *Ideology and Opinions: Studies in Rhetorical Psychology* (London).

Billig, M. (1996) *Arguing and Thinking* 2nd edn (1st edn 1987) (Cambridge).

Billington, S. (2015) *A Social History of the Fool*, rev. edn (1st edn 1984) London.

Blacking, J. (1987) *A Commonsense View of All Music* (Cambridge).

Bloch, M. (2008) 'Why Religion is Nothing Special but is Central', *Philosophical Transactions of the Royal Society B Biological Sciences* 363 (1499): 2055–61.

Bloch, M. (2012) *Anthropology and the Cognitive Challenge* (Cambridge).

Bloom, A.H. (1981) *The Linguistic Shaping of Thought. A Study in the Impact of Language on Thinking in China and the West* (Hillsdale, NJ).

Boas, F. (1901) 'The Mind of Primitive Man', *The Journal of American Folklore* 14 (52): 1–11.

Boas, F. (1930) *The Religion of the Kwakiutl Indians*, Part 2, Columbia University Contributions to Anthropology 10 (New York).

Boesch, C. (1996) 'The Emergence of Cultures in Wild Chimpanzees', in Runciman, Maynard Smith, and Dunbar (1996), 251–68.

Boesch, C. and Boesch, H. (1984) 'Possible Causes of Sex Differences in the Use of Natural Hammers by Wild Chimpanzees', *Journal of Human Evolution* 13: 415–40.

Bohannan, P. (1957) *Justice and Judgment among the Tiv* (Oxford).

Bourdieu, P. (2004) *Science of Science and Reflexivity* (trans. R. Nice of *Science de la science et réflexivité*, Paris 2001) (Cambridge).

Bowen, A.C. (2001) 'La scienza del cielo nel periodo pretolemaico', in S. Petruccioli (ed.) *Storia della scienza*, vol. 1 of *Enciclopedia Italiana* (Rome) section 4, ch. 21, 806–39.

Bowen, A.C. (2002) 'Simplicius and the Early History of Greek Planetary Theory', *Perspectives on Science* 10: 155–67.

Boyd, R. and Richerson, P.J. (2005) *The Origin and Evolution of Cultures* (Oxford).

Boyd, R., Richerson, P.J., and Henrich, J. (2011) 'The Cultural Niche: Why Social Learning is Essential for Human Adaptation', *Proceedings of the National Academy of Sciences* 108 (Suppl. 2) 10918–25.

Boyer, P. (1986) 'The "Empty" Concepts of Traditional Thinking', *Man* 21: 50–64.

Boyer, P. (ed.) (1993) *Cognitive Aspects of Religious Symbolism* (Cambridge).

Boyer, P. (1994) *The Naturalness of Religious Ideas: A Cognitive Theory of Religion* (Berkeley, CA).

Boyer, P. (1996) 'What Makes Anthropomorphism Natural? Intuitive Ontology and Cultural Representations', *Journal of the Royal Anthropological Institute* NS 2.1: 83–97.

Boyer, P. (2001) *Religion Explained* (New York).

Boyer, P. (2010) 'Why Evolved Cognition Matters to Understanding Cultural Cognitive Variations', *Interdisciplinary Science Reviews* 35: 376–86.

Boyer, P. and Baumard, N. (2018) 'The Diversity of Religious Systems across History', in J.R. Liddle and T.K. Shackelford (eds) *The Oxford Handbook of Evolutionary Psychology and Religion* (Oxford) pp. 1–24.

Bray, F., Dorofeeva-Lichtmann, V., and Métailié, G. (eds) (2007) *Graphics and Text in the Production of Technical Knowledge in China: The Warp and the Weft* (Leiden).

Bronkhorst, J. (2002) 'Discipliné par le débat', in L. Bansat-Boudon and J. Scheid (eds) *Le Disciple et ses maîtres* (Paris) pp. 207–25.

Bronkhorst, J. (2007) 'Modes of Debate and Refutation of Adversaries in Classical and Medieval India: A Preliminary Investigation', *Antiquorum Philosophia* 1: 269–80.

Brunschwig, J. (1980) 'Du mouvement et de l'immobilité de la loi', *Revue internationale de philosophie* 133–4: 512–40.

Burkert, W. (1985) *Greek Religion* (trans. J. Raffan of *Griechische Religion der archaischen und klassischen Epoche*, Stuttgart, 1977) (Oxford).

Burnyeat, M. (2000) 'Plato on Why Mathematics is Good for the Soul', in T. Smiley (ed.) *Mathematics and Necessity* (Proceedings of the British Academy 103) (Oxford) pp. 1–81.

Burnyeat, M. (2005) '*Eikōs Muthos*', *Rhizai* 2: 143–65.

Buxton, R.G.A. (ed.) (1999) *From Myth to Reason? Studies in the Development of Greek Thought* (Oxford).

Byrne, R.W. and Whiten, A. (eds) (1988) *Machiavellian Intelligence* (Oxford).

Caillois, R. (1961) *Man, Play and Games* (trans. M. Barash of *Les Jeux et les hommes* Paris 1958) (New York).

Calame, C. (1999) 'The Rhetoric of *Muthos* and *Logos*: Forms of Figurative Discourse', in Buxton (1999) pp. 119–43.

Carey, S. (1985) *Conceptual Change in Childhood* (Cambridge, MA).

Carey, S. (2009) *The Origin of Concepts* (Oxford).

Carey, S. and Spelke, E. (1994) 'Domain-specific Knowledge and Conceptual Change', in Hirschfeld and Gelman (1994) pp. 169–200.

Carneiro da Cunha, M. (2009) *'Culture' and Culture: Traditional Knowledge and Intellectual Rights* (Chicago).

Carruthers, P. (1996) *Language, Thought and Consciousness* (Cambridge).

Carruthers, P. (2008) 'Metacognition in Animals: A Skeptical Look', *Mind and Language* 23: 58–89.

Cartledge, P. (2009) *Ancient Greek Political Thought in Practice* (Cambridge).

Cartledge, P. (2016) *Democracy: A Life* (Oxford).

Catchpole, C.K. and Slater, P.J.B. (2008) *Bird Song*, 2nd edn (1st edn 1995) (Cambridge).

Changeux, J.-P. (1985) *Neuronal Man* (trans. L. Garey of *L'Homme neuronal*, Paris 1983) (New York).

Charbonnier, P., Salmon, G., and Skafish, P. (eds) (2017) *Comparative Metaphysics: Ontology after Anthropology* (London).

Chemla, K. (ed.) (2012) *The History of Mathematical Proof in Ancient Traditions* (Cambridge).

Chemla, K. and Guo, Shuchun, (2004) *Les Neuf chapitres. Le Classique mathématique de la Chine ancienne et ses commentaires* (Paris).

Cheney, D.L. and Seyfarth, R.M. (1990) *How Monkeys See the World* (Chicago).

Chomsky, N. (2006) *Language and Mind* 3rd edn (1st edn 1968) (Cambridge).

Clark, A. (2008) *Supersizing the Mind: Embodiment, Action and Cognitive Extension* (Oxford).

Clark, A. and Chalmers, D.J. (2010) 'The Extended Mind', in R. Menary (ed.), *The Extended Mind* (Cambridge, MA) (orig: *Analysis* (1998) 58.1: 7–19) 27–43.

Clunas, C. (1991) *Superfluous Things* (Cambridge).

Clunas, C. (1997) *Pictures and Visuality in Early Modern China* (London).

Cohen, H. Floris (1994) *The Scientific Revolution: A Historiographical Inquiry* (Chicago).

Cohen, H. Floris (2015) *The Rise of Modern Science Explained: A Comparative History* (Cambridge).

Cole, M., Gay, J., Glick, J.A., and Sharp, D.W. (1971) *The Cultural Context of Learning and Thinking* (New York).

Collins, D. (2008) *Magic in the Ancient Greek World* (Oxford).

Conklin, H.C. (1955) 'Hanunoo Color Terms', *Southwestern Journal of Anthropology* 11: 339–44.

Cooper, W.S. (2001) *The Evolution of Reason: Logic as a Branch of Biology* (Cambridge).

Cosmides, L. and Tooby, J, (1992) 'Cognitive Adaptations for Social Exchange', in Barkow, Cosmides, and Tooby (1992) pp. 163–228.

Crain, S. (2012) *The Emergence of Meaning* (Cambridge).

Crombie, A.C. (1994) *Styles of Scientific Thinking in the European Tradition* 3 vols (London).

Crump, T. (1990) *The Anthropology of Numbers* (Cambridge).

Crystal, D. (2002) *Language Death* (Cambridge).

Cullen, C. (1996) *Astronomy and Mathematics in Ancient China; The Zhou Bi Suan Jing* (Cambridge).

Cullen, C. (2007) 'Actors, Networks and "Disturbing Spectacles" in Institutional Science: 2nd Century Chinese Debates on Astronomy', *Antiquorum Philosophia* 1: 237–67.

Cuomo, S. (2001) *Ancient Mathematics* (London).

Curry, O.S., Mullins, D.A., and Whitehouse, H. (2019) 'Is it Good to Cooperate? Testing the Theory of Morality-as-Cooperation in 60 Societies' *Current Anthropology* 60.1: 47–69.

Daly, L. and Shepard, G. (2019) 'Magic Darts and Messenger Molecules', *Anthropology Today* 35.2: 13–17.

Damasio, A. (2018) *The Strange Order of Things* (New York).

D'Ambrosio, U. (1997) 'Etnomatematica', in A.B. Powell and M. Frankenstein (eds) *Mathematical Education* (Albany, NY) pp. 13–24.

D'Ambrosio, U. (2006) *Ethnomathematics: Link between Traditions and Modernity* (Rotterdam).

Darwin, C. (1859) *The Origin of Species* (London).

Darwin, C. (1871) *The Descent of Man* (London).

Daston, L. and Galison, P. (2007) *Objectivity* (New York).

Daston, L. and Lunbeck, E. (eds) (2011) *Histories of Scientific Observation* (Chicago).

Daston, L. and Mitman, G. (eds) (2005) *Thinking with Animals: New Perspectives on Anthropomorphism* (New York).

Davidson, D. (2001) *Essays on Actions and Events* 2nd edn (1st edn 1980) (Oxford).

Davidson, D. (2004) *Problems of Rationality* (Oxford).

Dawkins, R. (2006) *The God Delusion* (New York).

Dediu, D. and Levinson, S.C. (2018) 'Neanderthal Language Revisited: Not Only Us', *Current Opinion in Behavioral Sciences* 21: 49–55.

Dehaene, S. (2011) *The Number Sense: How the Mind Creates Mathematics*, rev. edn (orig. 1997) (Oxford).

De Jong, W.R. and Betti, A. (2010) 'The Classical Model of Science: A Millennia-Old Model of Scientific Rationality', *Synthèse* 174,2: 185–203.

Dennett, D.C. (2006) *Breaking the Spell: Religion as a Natural Phenomenon* (London).

Descola, P. (1996) *The Spears of Twilight* (trans. J. Lloyd of *Les Lances du crépuscule*, Paris 1993) (London).

Descola, P. (ed.) (2010) *La Fabrique des images* (Paris).

Descola, P. (2013) *Beyond Nature and Culture* (trans. J. Lloyd of *Par delà nature et culture*, Paris 2005) (Chicago).

Detienne, M. and Vernant, J.-P. (1978) *Cunning Intelligence in Greek Culture and Society* (trans. J. Lloyd of *Les Ruses de l'intelligence: La Mètis des grecs*, Paris 1974) (Hassocks).

Diamond, J. (1997) *Guns, Germs and Steel* (London).

Dias, M., Roazzi, A. and Harris, P.L. (2005) 'Reasoning from Unfamiliar Premises: a Study with Unschooled Adults', *Psychological Science* 16.7: 550–4.

Dodds, E.R. (1951) *The Greeks and the Irrational* (Berkeley CA).

Donald, M. (1991) *Origins of the Modern Mind* (Cambridge, MA).

Donald, M. (2001) *A Mind so Rare: the evolution of human consciousness* (New York).

Dor, D. and Jablonka, E. (2001) 'How Language Changed the Genes: Toward an Explicit Account of the Evolution of Language', in J. Trabant and S. Ward (eds) *New Essays on the Origin of Language* (Berlin), pp. 147–73.

Douglas, M. (1966) *Purity and Danger* (London).

Dunbar, R.I.M. (1998) 'The Social Brain Hypothesis', *Evolutionary Anthropology* 6: 178–90.

Dunbar, R.I.M. (1999) 'Culture, Honesty and the Freerider Problem', in R. Dunbar, C. Knight and C. Power (eds) *The Evolution of Culture* (Edinburgh), pp. 194–213.

Dunbar, R.I.M. (2009) 'The Social Brain Hypothesis and its Implications for Social Evolution', *Annals of Human Biology* 36,5: 562–72.

Dunn, J. (ed.) (1992) *Democracy: The Unfinished Journey* (Oxford).

Dunn, J. (2006) *Democracy: A History* (Oxford).

Dunn, J. (2018) *Setting the People Free: The Story of Democracy* 2nd edn (Oxford).

Dupré, J. (2002) *Humans and Other Animals* (Oxford).

Edelstein, E.J. and Edelstein, L. (1945) *Asclepius* 2 vols (Baltimore, MD).

Eisenstadt, S.N. (1982) 'The Axial Age: The Emergence of Transcendental Visions and the Rise of Clerics', *Archives Européennes de Sociologie* 23: 294–314.

Eisenstadt, S.N. (ed.) (1986) *The Origins and Diversity of Axial Age Civilizations* (Albany, NY).

Evans, E.P. (1906) *The Criminal Prosecution and Capital Punishment of Animals* (London).

Evans, J. (1998) *The History and Practice of Ancient Astronomy* (Oxford).

Evans, J. St.B.T. (1989) *Bias in Human Reasoning: Causes and Consequences* (Hove).

Evans, N. and Levinson, S.C. (2009) 'The Myth of Language Universals: Language Diversity and Its Importance for Cognitive Science', *Behavioral and Brain Sciences* 32: 429–92.

Evans-Pritchard, E.E. (1937) *Witchcraft, Oracles and Magic among the Azande* (Oxford).

Evans-Pritchard, E.E. (1956) *Nuer Religion* (Oxford).

Everett, D.L. (2005) 'Cultural Constraints on Grammar and Cognition in Pirahã', *Current Anthropology* 46: 621–34 and 641–6.

Faraone, C.A. (1999) *Ancient Greek Love Magic* (Cambridge, MA)

Faraone, C.A. and Obbink, D. (eds) (1991) *Magika Hiera: Ancient Greek Magic and Religion* (Oxford).

Fauconnier, G. and Turner, M. (2002) *The Way We Think* (New York).

Fikentscher, W. (2004) *Modes of Thought: A Study in the Anthropology of Law and Religion* (1st edn 1995) (Tübingen).

Finley, M.I. (1983) *Politics in the Ancient World* (Cambridge).

Finley, M.I. (1985) *Democracy Ancient and Modern*, rev. edn (1st edn 1973) (New Brunswick).

Fischhoff, B. (1975) 'Hindsight ≠ Foresight. The Effect of Outcome Knowledge on Judgment under Uncertainty', *Journal of Experimental Psychology: Human Perception and Performance* 1: 288–99.

Fortes, M. and Evans-Pritchard, E.E. (eds) (1940) *African Political Systems* (Oxford).

Fowler, R.L. (2011) 'Mythos and Logos', *Journal of Hellenic Studies* 131: 45–66.

Frazer, J.G. (1906–15) *The Golden Bough* 3rd edn 12 vols (1st edn 2 vols 1890) (London).

Fried, M. (forthcoming) *A Cultural History of Mathematics*, vol. 1 (London).

Gagné, R., Goldhill, S.G., and Lloyd, G.E.R. (eds) (2019) *Regimes of Comparatism: Frameworks of Comparison in History, Religion and Anthropology* (Leiden).

Gardner, R.A., Gardner, B.T., and van Cantfort, T.E. (eds) (1989) *Teaching Sign Language to Chimpanzees* (Albany, NY).

Geertz, C. (1973) *The Interpretation of Cultures* (New York).

Gell, A. (1998) *Art and Agency: An Anthropological Theory* (Oxford)

Gellner, E. (1973) 'The Savage and the Modern Mind', in Horton and Finnegan (1973) pp. 162–81.

Gernet, J. (1985) *China and the Christian Impact* (trans. J. Lloyd of *Chine et christianisme*, Paris 1982) (Cambridge).

Gernet, L. (1917) *Recherches sur le développement de la pensée juridique et morale en Grèce* (Paris).

Gernet, L. (1955) *Droit et société dans la Grèce ancienne* (Paris).

Gernet, L. (1981) *The Anthropology of Ancient Greece* (trans. J. Hamilton and B. Nagy of *Anthropologie de la Grèce antique*, Paris 1968) (Baltimore, MD).

Gigerenzer, G. (1996) 'On Narrow Norms and Vague Heuristics. A Reply to Kahneman and Tversky (1996)', *Psychological Review* 103: 592–6.

Gigerenzer, G. (2004) 'Fast and Frugal Heuristics: The Tools of Bounded Rationality', in D.J. Koehler and N. Harvey (eds) *Blackwell Handbook of Judgment and Decision Making* (Oxford) pp. 62–88.

Gigerenzer, G. (2007) *Gut Feelings: Short Cuts to Better Decision Making* (London).

Gigerenzer, G. and Brighton, H. (2009) 'Homo Heuristicus: Why Biased Minds Make Better Inferences', *Topics in Cognitive Science* 1: 107–43.

Gigerenzer, G. and Goldstein, D.G. (1996) 'Reasoning the Fast and Frugal Way: Models of Bounded Rationality', *Psychological Review* 103: 650–69.

Gigerenzer, G. and Todd, P.M. (1999) *Simple Heuristics That Make Us Smart* (Oxford).

Gluckman, M. (1965) *Politics, Law and Ritual in Tribal Society* (Oxford).

Gluckman, M. (1967) *The Judicial Process among the Barotse of Northern Rhodesia* 2nd edn (1st edn 1955) (Manchester).

Gluckman, M. (1972) *The Ideas in Barotse Jurisprudence* 2nd edn (1st edn 1965) (Manchester).

Godfrey-Smith, P. (1996) *Complexity and the Function of Mind in Nature* (Cambridge).

Godfrey-Smith, P. (2016) *Other Minds: The Octopus and the Evolution of Intelligent Life* (London).

Goodall, J. (1986) *The Chimpanzees of Gombe* (Cambridge, MA).

Goodman, N. (1978) *Ways of Worldmaking* (Hassocks).

Goody, J. (1961) 'Religion and Ritual: the definitional problem', *British Journal of Sociology* 12: 142–64.

Goody, J. (1977) *The Domestication of the Savage Mind* (Cambridge).

Goody, J. (1986) *The Logic of Writing and the Organization of Society* (Cambridge).

Gordon, P. (2004) 'Numerical Cognition without Words: Evidence from Amazonia', *Science* 306 (5695): 496–9.

Graf, F. (1999) *Magic in the Ancient World* (Cambridge, MA).

Grafton, A. (2019) 'Comparisons Compared: A Study in the Early Modern Roots of Cultural History', in Gagné, Goldhill, and Lloyd (2019) pp. 18–48.

Graham, A.C. (1978) *Later Mohist Logic, Ethics and Science* (London).

Graham, A.C. (1981) *Chuang-tzu: the Seven Inner Chapters* (London).

Graham, A.C. (1989) *Disputers of the Tao* (La Salle, IL).

Grice, H.P. (1968) 'Utterer's Meaning, Sentence-meaning, and Word-meaning', *Foundations of Language* 4: 225–42 (reprinted in Grice 1989: 117–37).

Grice, H.P. (1975) 'Logic and Conversation', in P. Cole and J. Morgan (eds) *Syntax and Semantics* vol. 3 *Speech Acts* (New York) pp. 41–58 (reprinted in Grice 1989: 22–40).

Grice, H.P. (1978) 'Further Notes on Logic and Conversation', in P. Cole *Syntax and Semantics* vol. 9 *Pragmatics* (New York) pp. 113–27 (reprinted in Grice 1989: 41–57).

Grice, H.P. (1989) *Studies in the Way of Words* (Cambridge, MA).

Griffin, D.R. (1984) *Animal Thinking* (Cambridge, MA).

Griffin, D.R. (1992) *Animal Minds* (Chicago).

Gumperz, J.J. and Levinson, S.C. (eds) (1996) *Rethinking Linguistic Relativity* (Cambridge).

Guthrie, S.E. (1993) *Faces in the Clouds: A New Theory of Religion* (Oxford).

Haas, J. (ed.) (1990) *The Anthropology of War* (Cambridge).

Hacking, I. (1992) '"Style" for Historians and Philosophers', *Studies in History and Philosophy of Science* 23,1: 1–20.

Hacking, I. (2009) *Scientific Reason* (Taipei).

Hacking, I. (2012) '"Language, Truth and Reason" 30 Years Later', *Studies in History and Philosophy of Science* 43.4: 599–609.

Hacking, I. (2014) *Why is There Philosophy of Mathematics at All?* (Cambridge).

Hankinson, R.J. (1991) 'Galen on the Foundations of Science', in J.A. López Férez (ed.) *Galeno: obra, pensamiento y influencia* (Madrid) pp. 15–29.

Hansen, M.H. (1983) *The Athenian Ecclesia* (Copenhagen).

Hansen, M.H. (1991) *The Athenian Democracy in the Age of Demosthenes* (Oxford).

Haraway, D. (2008) *When Species Meet* (Minneapolis).

Harbsmeier, C. (1998) *Science and Civilisation in China* vol. 7 part 1, *Language and Logic* (Cambridge).

Harman, G. (1986) *Change in View: Principles of Reasoning* (Cambridge, MA).

Harper, D. (1998) *Early Chinese Medical Literature: The Mawangdui Medical Manuscripts* (London).

Hartog, F. (1988) *The Mirror of Herodotus* (trans. J. Lloyd of *Le Miroir d'Hérodote*, Paris 1980) (Berkeley CA).

Hasse, H. and Scholz, H. (1928) *Die Grundlagenkrisis der griechischen Mathematik* (Berlin).

Hauser, M. (2006) *Moral Minds* (New York).

Havelock, E. (1982) *The Literate Revolution in Greece and Its Cultural Consequences* (Princeton).

Henare, A., Holbraad, M., and Wastell, S. (eds) (2007) *Thinking Through Things* (London).

Henrich, J. (2015) *The Secret of Our Success. How Culture is Driving Human Evolution, Domesticating Our Species and Making Us Smarter* (Princeton, NJ).

Henrich, J., Heine, S.J., and Norenzayan, A. (2010) 'The Weirdest People in the World?', *Behavioral and Brain Sciences* 33: 61–83.

Herzog, R. (1931) *Die Wunderheilungen von Epidauros* (Philologus Supp. Bd. 22.3) (Leipzig).

Hesse, M.B. (1963) *Models and Analogies in Science* (London).

Hinde, R.A. (ed.) (1992) *The Institution of War* (New York).

Hinde, R.A. (1999) *Why Gods Persist: A Scientific Approach to Religion* (London).

Hirschfeld, L.A., and Gelman, S.A. (eds) (1994) *Mapping the Mind: Domain Specificity in Cognition and Culture* (Cambridge).

Hodder, I. (1995) *Theory and Practice in Archaeology*, rev. edn (1st edn 1992) (London).

Hodder, I. (2018a) *Where Are We Heading? The Evolution of Humans and Things* (New Haven, CT).

Hodder, I. (ed.) (2018b) *Religion, History and Place in the Origin of Settled Life* (Boulder, CO).

Holbraad, M. and Pedersen, M.A. (2017) *The Ontological Turn: An Anthropological Exposition* (Cambridge).

Holbraad, M., Pedersen, M.A., and Viveiros de Castro, E. (2014) 'The Politics of Ontology: Anthropological Perspectives', *Cultural Anthropology* 13.

Hollis, M. (1987) *The Cunning of Reason* (Cambridge).

Hollis, M. and Lukes, S. (eds) (1982) *Rationality and Relativism* (Oxford).

Horton, R. (1960) 'A Definition of Religion and Its Uses', *Journal of the Royal Anthropological Institute of Great Britain and Ireland* 90: 201–26.

Horton, R. (1993) *Patterns of Thought in Africa and the West* (Cambridge).

Horton, R. and Finnegan, R. (eds) (1973) *Modes of Thought* (London).

Høyrup, J. (1994) *In Measure, Number and Weight* (Albany, NY).

Høyrup, J. (2002) *Lengths, Widths, Surfaces: A Portrait of Old Babylonian Algebra and its Kin* (New York).

Hsu, E. (2010) *Pulse Diagnosis in Early Chinese Medicine: The Telling Touch* (Cambridge).

Huff, T.E. (2011) *Intellectual Curiosity and the Scientific Revolution: A Global Perspective* (Cambridge).

Huffman, C. (1993) *Philolaus of Croton: Pythagorean and Presocratic* (Cambridge).

Huffman, C. (2005) *Archytas of Tarentum: Pythagorean, Philosopher and Mathematician King* (Cambridge).

Hugh-Jones, C. (1979) *From the Milk River* (Cambridge).

Hugh-Jones, S. (1979) *The Palm and the Pleiades* (Cambridge).

Hugh-Jones, S. (1994) 'Shamans, Prophets, Priests and Pastors', in N. Thomas and C. Humphrey (eds) *Shamanism, History, and the State* (Ann Arbor, MI) pp. 32–75.

Hugh-Jones, S. (2016) 'Writing on Stone; Writing on Paper: Myth, History and Memory in NW Amazonia', *History and Anthropology* 27: 154–82.

Hugh-Jones, S. (2017) 'Body Tubes and Synaesthesia', *Mundo Amazónico* 8,1: 27–78.

Hugh-Jones, S. (2019) 'Rhetorical Antinomies and Radical Othering', in Lloyd and Vilaça (2019) ch. 11.

Huizinga, J. (1970) *Homo Ludens* (trans. R.F.C. Hull of 1944 German edn (original Dutch edn 1938)), 2nd edn (London).

Hulsewé, A.F.P. (1955) *Remnants of Han Law: i Introductory Studies* (Leiden).

Humboldt, W. von (1988) *On Language: The Diversity of Human Language-structure and Its Influence on the Mental Development Of Mankind* (trans. P. Heath of *Über die Verschiedenheit des menschlichen Sprachbaues und ihren Einfluss auf die geistige Entwickelung des Menschengeschlechts*, Berlin 1836) (Cambridge).

Humle, T. and Matsuzawa, T. (2002) 'Ant-dipping among the Chimpanzees of Bossou, Guinea, and Some Comparisons With Other Sites', *American Journal of Primatology* 58: 133–48.

Humphrey, N. (1976) 'The Social Function Of Intellect', in P.P.G. Bateson and R.A. Hinde (eds) *Growing Points in Ethology* (Cambridge) pp. 303–17.

Humphrey, N. (1992) *A History of the Mind* (London).

Hutchins, E. (1995) *Cognition in the Wild* (Cambridge: MA).

Imhausen, A. (2009) 'Traditions and Myths in the Historiography of Egyptian Mathematics', in Robson and Stedall (2009) ch. 9.1: 781–800.

Ingold, T. (2000) *The Perception of the Environment* (London).

Jablonka, E. and Lamb, M.J. (2014) *Evolution in Four Dimensions* 2nd edn (1st edn 2005) (Cambridge, MA).

Jackendoff, R. (1996) 'How Language Helps Us Think', *Pragmatics and Cognition* 4: 1–34.

James, W. (1902) *The Varieties of Religious Experience* (London).

Jaspers, K. (1953) *The Origin and Goal of History* (trans. M. Bullock of *Vom Ursprung und Ziel der Geschichte*, Munich 1949) (London).

Johnson-Laird, P.N. (2006) *How We Reason* (Oxford).

Johnson-Laird, P.N., Legrenzi, P., and Legrenzi, M.S. (1972) 'Reasoning and a Sense of Reality', *The British Journal of Psychology* 63: 395–400.

Johnston, I. (2010) *The Mozi* (Hong Kong).

Johnston, S.I. (ed.) (2004) *Religions in the Ancient World* (Cambridge: MA).

Johnston, S.I. (2008) *Ancient Greek Divination* (Oxford).

Johnston, S.I. (2015) 'The Greek Mythic Story World', *Arethusa* 48.3: 283–311.

Kahn, C.H. (1973) *The Verb 'Be' in Ancient Greek*, Foundations of Language Suppl. 16 (Dordrecht).

Kahneman, D. (2011) *Thinking Fast and Slow* (London).

Kahneman, D. and Tversky, A. (1996) 'On the Reality of Cognitive Illusions', *Psychological Review* 103: 582–91.

Kahneman, D., Slovic, P., and Tversky, A. (eds) (1982) *Judgment under Uncertainty: Heuristics and Biases* (Cambridge).

Keane, W. (1997) 'Religious Language', *Annual Review of Anthropology* 26: 47–71.

Keane, W. (2008) 'The Evidence of the Senses and the Materiality of Religion', *Journal of the Royal Anthropological Institute* 14.1: S 110–27.

Keane, W. (2015) *Ethical Life: its Natural and Social Histories* (Princeton, NJ).

Keller, E.F. (2000) *The Century of the Gene* (Cambridge, MA).

Kirk, G.S. (1970) *Myth: Its Meaning and Functions in Ancient and Other Cultures* (Berkeley, CA).

Knoblock, J. (1988–94) *Xunzi: A Translation and Study of the Complete Works* 3 vols (Stanford, CA).

Knoblock, J. and Riegel, J. (2000) *The Annals of Lü Buwei* (Stanford, CA).

Kopenawa, D. and Albert, B. (2013) *The Falling Sky* (trans. N. Elliot of *La Chute du ciel*, Paris 2010) (Minnesota).

Koselleck, R. (1985) *Futures Past: On the Semantics of Historical Time* (trans. K. Tribe) (Cambridge, MA).

Kroeber, A.L. and Kluckhohn, C. (1952) *Culture: A Critical Review of Concepts and Definitions* (Peabody Museum of American Archaeology and Ethnology 47, Cambridge MA).

Kuhn, T.S. (1970) *The Structure of Scientific Revolutions* 2nd edn (1st edn 1962) (Chicago).

Kuhn, T.S. (1977) *The Essential Tension* (Chicago).

Kuper, A. (1999) *Culture: The Anthropologists' Account* (Cambridge, MA).

Ladefoged, P. (1992) 'Another View of Endangered Languages', *Language* 68.4: 809–11.

Laidlaw, J. (2017) Review of Holbraad and Pedersen 2017, *Current Anthropology* 25: 396–402.

Laidlaw, J. and Heywood, P. (2013) 'One More Turn and You're There', *Anthropology of This Century* 7.

Lang, P. (ed.) (2004) *Reinventions: Essays on Hellenistic and Early Roman Science* (Kelowna, BC).

Latour, B. (2009) 'Perspectivism: "Type" or "Bomb"?', *Anthropology Today* 25.2: 1–2.

Latour, B. (2013) *An Inquiry into Modes of Existence* (trans. C. Porter of *Enquête sur les modes d'existence*, Paris 2012) (Cambridge, MA).

Lave, J. (1988) *Cognition in Practice: Mind, Mathematics and Culture in Everyday Life* (Cambridge).

Leach, E. (1954) 'Aesthetics', in E.E. Evans-Pritchard et al. (eds) *The Institutions of Primitive Society* (Oxford) ch. 3: 25–33.

Lear, J. (1982) 'Aristotle's Philosophy of Mathematics', *Philosophical Review* 91: 161–92.

Leavitt, J. (2011) *Linguistic Relativities: Language Diversity and Modern Thought* (Cambridge).

LeGoff, J. (1974) 'Les mentalités: une histoire ambiguë', in *Faire de l'histoire*, ed. J. LeGoff and P. Nora vol. 3 (Paris) pp. 76–94.

Levinson, S.C. (2003) *Space in Language and Cognition* (Cambridge).

Levinson, S.C. (2005) 'Comments on Everett (2005)', *Current Anthropology* 46: 637–8.

Levinson, S.C. and Jaisson, P. (eds) (2006). *Evolution and Culture* (Cambridge, MA).

Lévi-Strauss, C. (1966) *The Savage Mind* (trans. of *La Pensée sauvage*, Paris 1962) (London).

Lévi-Strauss, C. (1968) *Structural Anthropology* (trans. C. Jacobson and B.G. Schoepf of *Anthropologie structurale*, Paris 1958) (London).

Lévi-Strauss, C. (1969) *Totemism* (trans. R. Needham of *Le Totémisme aujourd'hui*, Paris 1962) (London).

Lévi-Strauss, C. (1970–81) *Introduction to the Science of Mythology* (trans. J. and D. Weightman of *Mythologiques*, Paris 1964–71) 4 vols (London).

Lévi-Strauss, C. (1973) *The World on the Wane* (trans. J. and D. Weightman of *Tristes Tropiques*, Paris 1955) (London).

Lévi-Strauss, C. (1976) *Structural Anthropology II* (trans. M. Layton of *Anthropologie structurale deux*, Paris 1973) (New York).

Levitin, D. (2015) *Ancient Wisdom in the Age of the New Science* (Cambridge).

Levitin, D. (2019) 'What Was the Comparative History of Religions in 17th- century Europe (and Beyond)? Pagan Monotheism/pagan Animism from *T'ien* to Tylor', in Gagné, Goldhill, and Lloyd (2019) pp. 49–115.

Lévy-Bruhl, L. (1923) *Primitive Mentality* (trans. L.A. Clare of *La Mentalité primitive*, Paris 1922) (New York).

Lévy-Bruhl, L. (1926) *How Natives Think* (trans. L.A. Clare of *Les Fonctions mentales dans les sociétés inférieures*, Paris 1910) (London).

Lévy-Bruhl, L. (1975) *The Notebooks on Primitive Mentality* (trans. P. Rivière of *Les Carnets de Lucien Lévy-Bruhl*, Paris 1949) (London).

Lewis, D. (1994) *We the Navigators* 2nd edn (1st edn 1972) (Honolulu).

LiDonnici, L.R. (1995) *The Epidaurian Miracle Inscriptions: Text, Translation and Commentary* (Atlanta, GA).

Lienhardt, G. (1961) *The Religion of the Dinka* (Oxford).

Lloyd, G.E.R. (1966) *Polarity and Analogy* (Cambridge).

Lloyd, G.E.R. (1979) *Magic, Reason and Experience* (Cambridge).

Lloyd, G.E.R. (1990) *Demystifying Mentalities* (Cambridge).

Lloyd, G.E.R. (1991) *Methods and Problems in Greek Science* (Cambridge).

Lloyd, G.E.R. (1996a) *Adversaries and Authorities* (Cambridge).

Lloyd, G.E.R. (1996b) *Aristotelian Explorations* (Cambridge).

Lloyd, G.E.R. (2000) 'On the "Origins" of Science', *Proceedings of the British Academy*, 105: 1–16.

Lloyd, G.E.R. (2002) *The Ambitions of Curiosity* (Cambridge).

Lloyd, G.E.R. (2003) *In the Grip of Disease: Studies in the Greek Imagination* (Oxford).

Lloyd, G.E.R. (2005) 'The Institutions of Censure: China, Greece and the Modern World', *Quaderni di Storia* 62: 7–52.

Lloyd, G.E.R. (2006) *Principles and Practices in Ancient Greek and Chinese Science* (Aldershot).

Lloyd, G.E.R. (2007) *Cognitive Variations: Reflections on the Unity and Diversity of the Human Mind* (Oxford).

Lloyd, G.E.R. (2009) *Disciplines in the Making* (Oxford).

Lloyd, G.E.R. (2010) 'The Techniques of Persuasion and the Rhetoric of Disorder (*luan*) in Late Zhanguo and Western Han Texts', in M. Nylan and M.A.N. Loewe (eds) *China's Early Empires* (Cambridge) ch. 19: 451–60.

Lloyd, G.E.R. (2012a) *Being, Humanity, and Understanding* (Oxford).

Lloyd, G.E.R. (2012b) 'The Pluralism of Greek "Mathematics"', in Chemla (ed.) (2012) pp. 294–310.

Lloyd, G.E.R. (2013) 'Aristotle on the Natural Sociability, Skills and Intelligence of Animals', in V. Harte and M. Lane (eds) *Politeia in Greek and Roman Philosophy* (Cambridge) pp. 277–93.

Lloyd, G.E.R. (2014) *The Ideals of Inquiry* (Oxford).

Lloyd, G.E.R. (2015) *Analogical Investigations* (Cambridge).

Lloyd, G.E.R. (2018) *The Ambivalences of Rationality* (Cambridge).

Lloyd, G.E.R. and Sivin, N. (2002) *The Way and the Word* (New Haven, CT).

Lloyd, G.E.R. and Vilaça, A. (eds) (2019) 'Science in the Forest, Science in the Past', *HAU, Journal of Ethnographic Theory, Special Issue*.

Lloyd, G.E.R. and Zhao, J.J. (eds) (2017) *Ancient Greece and China Compared* (Cambridge).

Luhrmann, T. (2012) *When God Talks Back: Understanding the American Evangelical Relationship with God* (New York).

Luhrmann, T. (2020) *How God Becomes Real: Kindling the Presence of Invisible Others* (Princeton).

Lukes, S. (2000) 'Different Cultures, Different Rationalities?' *History of the Human Sciences* 13.1: 3–18.

Luria, A.R. (1976) *Cognitive Development: Its Cultural and Social Foundations* (Cambridge, MA).

Lyons, J. (1995) 'Colour in Language', in T. Lamb and J. Bourriau (eds) *Colour: Art and Science* (Cambridge) pp. 194–224.

McCarty, W. (2019) 'Modelling, Ontology and Wild Thought: Towards an Anthropology of the Artificially Intelligent', in Lloyd and Vilaça (2019) ch. 10.

McCarty, W., Lloyd, G.E.R., and Vilaça, A. (2021) 'Science in the Forest, Science in the Past Part II', *Interdisciplinary Science Reviews* 46.3.

McGrew, W.C. (1992) *Chimpanzee Material Culture* (Cambridge).

Major, J.S. (1993) *Heaven and Earth in Early Han Thought* (Albany, NY).

Major, J.S., Queen, S.A., Meyer, A.S., and Roth, A.D. (eds) (2010) *The Huainanzi: A Guide to the Theory and Practice of Government in Early Han China* (New York).

Malinowski, B. (1925) 'Magic Science and Religion', in J. Needham (ed.) *Science, Religion and Reality* (London) pp. 19–84.

Manser, M.B., Bell, M.B., and Fletcher, L.B. (2001) 'The Information the Receivers Extract from Alarm Calls in Suricates', *Proceeding of the Royal Society B Biological Sciences* 268 (1484): 2485–91.

Markus, H.R. and Kitayama, S. (1991) 'Culture and the Self: Implications for Cognition, Emotion, and Motivation', *Psychological Review* 98: 224–53.

Marshall, L. (1957) ' "N'ow" ', *Africa* 27: 232–40.

Martin, M. (2012) *La Magie dans l'antiquité* (Paris).

Martzloff, J.-C. (2006) *A History of Chinese Mathematics* (trans. S.S. Wilson of *Histoire des mathématiques chinoises*, Paris, 1988) 2nd edn (Berlin).

Matilal, B.K. (1985) *Logic, Language and Reality: an Introduction to Indian Philosophical Studies* (Delhi).

Matthews, G.B. (1984) *Dialogues with Children* (Cambridge, MA).

Matthews, G.B. (1994) *The Philosophy of Childhood* (Cambridge, MA).

Medin, D.L. and Atran, S. (eds) (1999) *Folkbiology* (Cambridge, MA).

Mehr, S.A. et al. (2018) 'A Natural History of Song' https://DOI.org/10.31234/osf.io/emq8r.

Meier, C.A. (2009) *Healing Dream and Rituals: Ancient Incubation and Modern Psychotherapy* (Einsiedeln, Switzerland).

Mercier, H. (2011) 'On the Universality of Argumentative Reasoning', *Journal of Cognition and Culture* 11.1: 85–113.

Mercier, H. and Sperber, D. (2011) 'Why Do Humans Reason? Arguments for an Argumentative Theory', *Behavioral and Brain Sciences* 34.2: 57–74.

Mercier, H. and Sperber, D. (2017) *The Enigma of Reason: A New Theory of Human Understanding* (London).

Merton, R.K. (1938) *Science, Technology and Society in Seventeenth Century England* (New York).

Merton, R.K. (1973) *The Sociology of Science* (Chicago).

Meyer, B. (2016) 'How to Capture the "Wow": R.R. Marett's Notion of Awe and the Study of Religion', *Journal of the Royal Anthropological Institute* 22: 7–26.

Milam, E.L. (2018) *Creatures of Cain* (Princeton, NJ).

Mohanty, J.N. (1992) *Reason and Tradition in Indian Thought* (Oxford).

Mol, A.-M. (2002) *The Body Multiple: Ontology in Medical Practice* (Durham, NC).

Neugebauer, O. (1975) *A History of Ancient Mathematical Astronomy* 3 vols (Berlin).

Netz, R. (1999) *The Shaping of Deduction in Greek Mathematics* (Cambridge).

Netz, R. (2009) *Ludic Proof* (Cambridge).

Netz, R. (2017) *The Works of Archimedes*, vol. 2, *On Spirals* (Cambridge).

Nickerson, R.S. (1998) 'Confirmation Bias: A Ubiquitous Phenomenon in Many Guises', *Review of General Psychology* 2: 175–220.

Nickerson, R.S. (2008) *Aspects of Rationality* (New York).

Nisbett, R.E. (2003) *The Geography of Thought: How Asians and Westerners Think Differently ... and Why* (New York).

Nisbett, R.E. and Ross, L. (1980) *Human Inference: Strategies and Shortcomings of Social Judgement* (Englewood Cliffs, NJ).

Norenzayan, A. (2013) *Big Gods: How Religion Transformed Cooperation and Conflict* (Princeton, NJ).

Norenzayan, A. and Heine, S.J. (2005) 'Psychological Universals: What are They and How Can We Know?', *Psychological Bulletin* 131.5: 763–84.

Nutton, V. (1988) *From Democedes to Harvey* (London).

Nutton, V. (2004) *Ancient Medicine* (London).

Nylan, M. (2001) *The Five 'Confucian' Classics* (New Haven, CT).

Ober, J. (1989) *Mass and Elite in Democratic Athens* (Princeton, NJ).

Olivelle, P. (1996) *Upaniṣads* (Oxford).

Olson, D.R. (1994) *The World on Paper* (Cambridge).

Olson, D.R. and Torrance, N. (eds) (1991) *Literacy and Orality* (Cambridge).

Olson, D.R. and Torrance, N. (eds) (1996) *Modes of Thought: Explorations in Culture and Cognition* (Cambridge).

Ong, W.J. (1977) *Interfaces of the Word: Studies in the Evolution of Consciousness and Culture* (Ithaca, NY).

Ong, W.J. (1982) *Orality and Literacy* (London).

Osborne, C. (2007) *Dumb Beasts and Dead Philosophers. Humanity and the Humane in Ancient Philosophy and Literature* (Oxford).

Osborne, R. (1997) 'The Polis and Its Culture', in C.C.W. Taylor (ed.). *From the Beginning to Plato: Routledge History of Philosophy* vol. 1 (London) pp. 9–46.

Osborne, R. (2007) *Debating the Athenian Cultural Revolution* (Cambridge).

Osborne, R. (2010) *Athens and Athenian Democracy* (Cambridge).

Ostwald, M. (1969) *Nomos and the Beginnings of the Athenian Democracy* (Oxford).

Parry, J.P. (1985) 'The Brahmanical Tradition and the Technology of the Intellect', in J. Overing (ed.), *Reason and Morality* (London) pp. 200–25.

Pedersen, M.A. (2012) 'Common Nonsense: A Review of Certain Recent Reviews of the Ontological Turn', *Anthropology of This Century* 5.

Piaget, J. (1929) *The Child's Conception of the World* (trans. J. and A. Tomlinson of *La Représentation du monde chez l'enfant*, Paris 1926) (London).

Piaget, J. (1930) *The Child's Conception of Physical Causality* (trans. M. Gabain of *La Causalité physique chez l'enfant*, Paris 1927) (London).

Piaget, J. (1959) *The Language and Thought of the Child*, rev. edn (trans. M. Gabain of *Le Langage et la pensée chez l'enfant*, Paris 1923) (London).

Pinker, S. (1994) *The Language Instinct* (New York).

Pinker, S. (1997) *How the Mind Works* (London).

Pollan, M. (2013) 'The Intelligent Plant', *The New Yorker* 89: 92–105.

Premack, D. (1976) *Intelligence in Ape and Man* (Hillsdale, NJ).

Premack, D. and Premack, A.J. (1983) *The Mind of an Ape* (New York).

Prets, E. (2000) 'Theories Of Debate, Proof and Counter-proof in the Early Indian Dialectical Tradition' (*Studia Indologiczne* 7) in Piotr Balcerowicz and M. Mejor (eds) *On the Understanding of Other Cultures* (Warsaw Oriental Institute) pp. 369–82.

Prets, E. (2001) 'Futile and False Rejoinders, Sophistical Arguments and Early Indian Logic', *Journal of Indian Philosophy* 29: 545–58.

Prets, E. (2003) 'Parley, Reason and Rejoinder', *Journal of Indian Philosophy* 31: 271–83

Priest, G. (2008) *An Introduction to Non-Classical Logic* 2nd edn (1st edn 2001) (Cambridge).

Priest, G., Routley, R. and Norman, J. (eds) (1989) *Paraconsistent Logic: Essays on the Inconsistent* (Munich).

Puett, M. J. (2002) *To Become a God: Cosmology, Sacrifice, and Self-Divinization in Early China* (Cambridge, MA).

Puett, M.J. (2017) 'Genealogies of Gods, Ghosts and Humans', in Lloyd and Zhao (2017) pp. 160–85.

Putnam, H. (1981) *Reason, Truth and History* (Cambridge).

Pyysiainen, I. (2001) *How Religion Works: Towards a New Cognitive Science of Religion* (Leiden).

Pyysiainen, I. and Anttonen, V. (eds) (2002) *Current Approaches in the Cognitive Science of Religion* (London).

Quine, W. van O. (1960) *Word and Object* (Cambridge, MA).

Quine, W. van O. (1969) *Ontological Relativity and Other Essays* (New York).

Rappaport, R.A. (1999) *Ritual and Religion in the Making of Humanity* (Cambridge).

Rees, M. (2001) *Our Cosmic Habitat* (Princeton, NJ).

Renfrew, C. and Zabrow, E.B.W. (eds) (1994) *The Ancient Mind: Elements of Cognitive Archaeology* (Cambridge).

Richerson, P.J. and Boyd, R. (2005) *Not by Genes Alone* (Chicago).

Rips, L.J. (1998) *The Psychology of Proof: Deductive Reasoning in Human Thinking* (Cambridge, MA).

Robbins, J. (2004) *Becoming Sinners: Christianity and moral torment in a Papua New Guinea Society* (Berkeley, CA).

Robson, E. (1999) *Mesopotamian Mathematics, 2100–1600 BC: Technical Constants in Bureaucracy and Education* (Oxford).

Robson, E. (2009) 'Mathematics Education in an Old Babylonian Scribal School', in Robson and Stedall (2009) ch. 3.1: 199–227.

Robson, E. and Stedall, J. (eds) (2009) *The Oxford Handbook of the History of Mathematics* (Oxford).

Rochberg, F. (2004) *The Heavenly Writing. Divination, Horoscopy and Astronomy in Mesopotamian Culture* (Cambridge).

Rochberg, F. (2016) *Before Nature. Cuneiform Knowledge and the History of Science* (Chicago).

Runciman, W.G. (1998) *The Social Animal* (London).

Runciman, W.G. (2009) *The Theory of Cultural and Social Selection* (Cambridge).

Runciman, W.G., Maynard Smith, J., and Dunbar, R.I.M. (eds) (1996) 'Evolution of Social Behaviour Patterns in Primates and Man', *Proceedings of the British Academy* 88.

Sahlins, M. (1995) *How 'Natives' Think, about Captain Cook, for Example* (Chicago).

Salmond, A. (2021) 'Star canoes, voyaging worlds', in McCarty, Lloyd and Vilaça (eds) (2021) pp. 267-85.

Sambursky, S. (1962) *The Physical World of Late Antiquity* (London).

Samuels, H., Stich, S., and Bishop, M. (2002) 'Ending the Rationality Wars', in R. Elio (ed.) *Common Sense, Reasoning and Rationality* (Oxford) pp. 236-68.

Sapir, E. (1949) *Selected Writings of Edward Sapir in Language, Culture, and Personality* (Berkeley, CA).

Schaberg, D. (1997) 'Remonstrance in Eastern Zhou Historiography', *Early China* 22: 133-79.

Schickore, J. (2017) *About Method: Experimenters, Snake Venom, and the History of Writing Scientifically* (Chicago).

Scoditti, G.M.G. (1990) *Kitawa: A Linguistic and Aesthetic Analysis of Visual Art in Melanesia* (Berlin).

Seaford, R. (2004) *Money and the Early Greek Mind* (Cambridge).

Searle, J.R. (2001) *Rationality in Action* (Cambridge, MA).

Sedley, D.N. (2007) *Creationism and its Critics in Antiquity* (Berkeley, CA).

Severi, C. (2013) 'Philosophies without Ontology', *HAU: Journal of Ethnographic Theory* 3: 192-6.

Seyfarth, R.M. and Cheney, D.L. (1982) 'How Monkeys See the World: A Review of Recent Research on East African Vervet Monkeys', in C.T. Snowdon, C.H. Brown, and M.R. Petersen (eds) *Primate Communication* (Cambridge), pp. 239-52.

Seyfarth, R.M. and Cheney, D.L. (1984) 'Grooming, Alliances and Reciprocal Altruism in Vervet Monkeys', *Nature* 308: 541-3.

Sivin, N. (1995a) *Science in Ancient China: Researches and Reflections* vol. 1 (Aldershot).

Sivin, N. (1995b) *Medicine, Philosophy and Religion in Ancient China: Researches and Reflections,* vol. 2 (Aldershot).

Sivin, N. (1995c) 'Text and Experience In Classical Chinese Medicine', in D. Bates (ed.) *Knowledge and the Scholarly Medical Traditions* (Cambridge) pp. 177-204.

Skinner, Q. (1966) 'The Limits of Historical Explanations', *Philosophy* 41: 199-215.

Skinner, Q. (1969) 'Meaning and Understanding in the History of Ideas', *History and Theory* 8: 3-53.

Skinner, Q. (1971) 'On Performing and Explaining Linguistic Actions', *Philosophical Quarterly* 21: 1-21.

Skinner, Q. (1975) 'Hermeneutics and the Role of History', *New Literary History* 7: 209–32.

Snell, B. (1953) *The Discovery of the Mind* (trans. T.G. Rosenmeyer of *Die Entdeckung des Geistes*, 2nd edn Hamburg 1948) (Oxford).

Snodgrass, A. (1965) 'The Hoplite Reform and History', *Journal of Hellenic Studies* 85: 110–22.

Sorabji, R. (1993) *Animal Minds and Human Morals* (London).

Sperber, D. (1975) *Rethinking Symbolism* (trans. A.L. Morton) (Cambridge).

Sperber, D. (1980) 'Is Symbolic Thought Pre-rational?', in M.L.Foster and S. H. Brandes (eds) *Symbol as Sense* (New York) pp. 25–44.

Sperber, D. (1985) *On Anthropological Knowledge* (Cambridge).

Sperber, D. (1996) *Explaining Culture: A Naturalistic Approach* (Oxford).

Sperber, D. (1997) 'Intuitive and Reflective Beliefs', *Mind and Language* 12.1: 67–83.

Sperber, D., Cara, F. and Girotto, V. (1995) 'Relevance Theory Explains the Selection Task', *Cognition* 57: 31–95.

Sperber, D., Premack, D., and Premack, A.J. (eds) (1995) *Causal Cognition: A Multidisciplinary Debate* (Oxford).

Sterckx, R. (2002) *The Animal and the Daemon in Early China* (Albany, NY).

Sterckx, R., Siebert, M., and Schäfer, D. (eds) (2019) *Animals Through Chinese History* (Cambridge).

Sternberg, R.J. and Kaufman, J.C. (eds) (2002) *The Evolution of Intelligence* (Hillsdale, NJ).

Strathern, M. (1980) 'No Nature, No Culture: The Hagen Case', in C.P. MacCormack and M. Strathern (eds) *Nature, Culture and Gender* (Cambridge) pp. 174–222.

Strathern, M. (1988) *The Gender of the Gift* (Berkeley, CA).

Strathern, M. (2019) 'A Clash of Ontologies? Time, Law and Science in Papua New Guinea', in Lloyd and Vilaça (2019) ch. 3.

Sturm, T. (2012) 'The "Rationality Wars" in Psychology: Where They are and Where They Could Go', *Inquiry* 55.1: 66–81.

Szabó, Á. (1978) *The Beginnings of Greek Mathematics* (trans. A.M. Ungar of *Anfänge der griechischen Mathematik*, Vienna 1969) (Budapest).

Tambiah, S.J. (1968) 'The Magical Power of Words', *Man* NS 3: 175–208.

Tambiah, S.J. (1973) 'Form and Meaning of Magical Acts: A Point of View', in Horton and Finnegan (1973) pp. 199–229.

Tambiah, S.J. (1985) *Culture, Thought and Social Action* (Cambridge, MA).

Tambiah, S.J. (1990) *Magic, Science, Religion and the Scope of Rationality* (Cambridge).

Taylor, A.-C. (2013) 'Distinguishing Ontologies', *HAU, Journal of Ethnographic Theory* 3: 201–4.

Teich, M. and Müller, M. (eds) (2005) *Historia Magistra Vitae?* (Österreichische Zeitschrift für Geschichtswissenschaften 16.2) (Innsbruck).

Thomas, K. (1971) *Religion and the Decline of Magic* (London).

Thomas, R. (2002) *Herodotus in Context: Ethnography, Science and the Art of Persuasion in Classical Athens*, rev. edn (Cambridge).

Tomasello, M. (1999) *The Cultural Origins of Human Cognition* (Cambridge: MA).

Tomasello, M. and Rakoczy, H. (2003) 'What Makes Human Cognition Unique? From Individual to Shared to Collective Intentionality', *Mind and Language* 18.2: 121–47.

Tooby, J. and Cosmides, L. (1989) 'Evolutionary Psychology and the Generation of Culture: Part I, Theoretical Considerations', *Ethology and Sociobiology* 10: 29–49.

Tooby, J. and Cosmides. L. (1990) 'The Past Explains the Present. Emotional Adaptations and the Structure of Ancestral Environments', *Ethology and Sociobiology* 11: 375–424.

Tooby, J. and Cosmides, L. (1992) 'The Psychological Foundations of Culture', in Barkow, Cosmides, and Tooby (1992) pp. 19–136.

Toomer, G.J. (1984) *Ptolemy's Almagest* (London).

Trehub, S.E., Unyk, A.M., and Trainor, L.J. (1993) 'Adults Identify Infant-directed Music across Cultures', *Infant Behavior and Development* 16.2: 193–211.

Tsing, A.L. (2015) *The Mushroom at the End of the World* (Princeton, NJ).

Turner, T. (2009) 'The Crisis of Late Structuralism. Perspectivism and Animism: Rethinking Culture, Nature, Spirit, and Bodiliness', *Tipití: The Journal of the Society for the Anthropology of Lowland South America* 7.1: 1–40.

Tversky, A. and Kahneman, D. (1974) 'Judgment under Uncertainty: Heuristics and Biases', *Science* 1974 NS 185: 1124–31 (reprinted in Kahneman, Slovic, and Tversky (1982) pp. 3–21).

Tybjerg, K. (2004) 'Hero of Alexandria's Mechanical Geometry', in Lang (2004) pp. 29–56.

Tylor, E.B. (1891) *Primitive Culture*, 2nd edn (1st edn 1871) 2 vols (London).

Urton, G. (1997) *The Social Life of Numbers* (Austin, TX).

Vanderpool, E. (1970) *Ostracism at Athens* (Cincinnati, OH).

Vernant, J.P. (1980) *Myth and Society in Ancient Greece* (trans. J. Lloyd of *Mythe et société en Grèce ancienne*, Paris 1974) (New York).

Vernant, J.P. (1983) *Myth and Thought among the Greeks* (trans. of *Mythe et pensée chez les grecs*, Paris 1965) (London).

Verran, H. (2001) *Science and an African Logic* (Chicago).

Verran, H. (2011) 'Comparison as Participant', *Common Knowledge* 17.1: 64–70.

Vilaça, A. (2010) *Strange Enemies: Indigenous Agency and Scenes of Encounters in Amazonia* (trans. D. Rodgers of *Quem somos nós: Os Wari' encontram os brancos*, Rio de Janeiro 2006) (Durham, NC).

Vilaça, A. (2019) 'Inventing Nature: Christianity and Science in Indigenous Amazonia', in Lloyd and Vilaça (2019) ch. 2.

Vilaça, A. (2021) 'A pagan arithmetic: unstable sets in indigenous Amazonia', in McCarty, Lloyd and Vilaça (eds) (2021) pp. 304-24.

Viveiros de Castro, E. (1992) *From the Enemy's Point of View* (Chicago).

Viveiros de Castro, E. (1998) 'Cosmological Deixis and Amerindian Perspectivism', *Journal of the Royal Anthropological Institute* NS 4: 469–88.

Viveiros de Castro, E. (2014) *Cannibal Metaphysics* (trans. P. Skafish of *Métaphysiques cannibales*, Paris 2009) (Minneapolis).

Viveiros de Castro, E. (2015) *The Relative Native: Essays on Indigenous Conceptual Worlds* (Chicago).

Vranas, P.B.M. (2000) 'Gigerenzer's Normative Critique of Kahneman and Tversky', *Cognition* 76: 179–93.

Vygotsky, L. (1986) *Thought and Language* (Cambridge MA).

Waal, F.B.M. de (1991) 'The Chimpanzee's Sense of Social Regularity and Its Relation to the Human Sense of Justice', *American Behavioral Scientist* 34: 335–49.

Waal, F.B.M. de (1996) *Good Natured* (Cambridge, MA).

Waal, F.B.M. de (1998) *Chimpanzee Politics*, rev. edn (1st edn 1982) (Baltimore, MD).

Wagner, R. (2016) *The Invention of Culture*, 2nd edn (1st edn 1975) (Chicago).

Wang, Y. (2017) 'Identifying the Beginnings of Sheep Husbandry in Western China' (PhD dissertation, University of Cambridge).

Wardhaugh, R. (2010) *An Introduction to Sociolinguistics*, 6th edn (Oxford).

Wason, P.C. (1966) 'Reasoning', in B.M. Foss (ed.) *New Horizons in Psychology* (Harmondsworth) pp. 135–51.

Wason, P.C. (1968) 'Reasoning about a Rule', *Quarterly Journal of Experimental Psychology* 20: 273–81.

Wason, P.C. and Johnson-Laird, P.N. (1972) *Psychology of Reasoning: Structure and Content* (London).

Watson, R. and Horowitz, W. (2011) *Writing Science before the Greeks* (Leiden).

Weber, M. (1930) *The Protestant Ethic and the Spirit of Capitalism*, trans. Talcott Parsons (London).

Weber, M. (1948) *From Max Weber: Essays in Sociology* (trans., ed., and intro. H. H. Gerth and C. Wright Mills) (London).

Whitehouse, H. (2000) *Arguments and Icons: Divergent Modes of Religiosity* (Oxford).

Whitehouse, H. (2004) *Modes of Religiosity: A Cognitive Theory of Religious Transmission* (Walnut Creek, CA).

Whiten, A. and Byrne, R.W. (eds) (1997) *Machiavellian Intelligence II* (Cambridge).

Whorf, B.L. (2012) *Language, Thought, and Reality*, 2nd edn J. Carroll, S.C. Levinson, and P. Lee (1st edn 1956) (Cambridge, MA).

Willis, R. and Curry, P. (2004) *Astrology, Science and Culture: Pulling Down the Moon* (Oxford).

Wilson, B.R. (ed.) (1970) *Rationality* (Oxford).

Wittgenstein, L. (1953) *Philosophical Investigations*, trans. G.E.M. Anscombe (Oxford).

Index

For the benefit of digital users, indexed terms that span two pages (e.g., 52–53) may, on occasion, appear on only one of those pages.

Kula 118
!Kung 22

language 13, 17, 30–39, 40, 43, 47–9,
    50–1, 55–6, 59, 95, 99, 110, 126, 128
  Chinese 32, 36
  English 32, 68, 95, 127
  French 32–3
  Greek 33, 36, 48, 109
  Latin 48, 95, 100
  Portuguese 72–3
Laozi 108n.1
law 41, 44, 107–15, 127
  unwritten 114
law-courts 14, 46
Leach, E. 116
Lévi-Strauss, C. 121
Levinson, S. 66–8
Lévy-Bruhl, L. 5–6, 129
literacy 5, 9, 16, 26
literal versus metaphorical 18–19,
    54, 126
Liu Hui 74–5
logic 5, 7, 9–10, 17, 63
  formal 8
logos 16, 78
Lun Heng 29n.9
Lunyu 27, 120
Luria, S. 6–7, 17
Lüshi chunqiu 47, 61

magic 5, 20–29, 95, 126
Magoi 20
Malinowski, B. 5, 21, 129
Marshall, L. 22
Marx, K. 98
matter 81, 89
meaning 13, 31, 99
'mechanics' 73, 83, 86
meditation 98
meerkats 30
Mencius (Mengzi) 48
mensuration 86
mentalities 5–6
metaphor 19, 54, 126, 129
metaphysics 53, 55, 78, 80, 111

methods 4, 10, 64, 127
mētis (cunning intelligence) 47n.6, 62
mind 6, 96, 121
missionaries 37, 52, 72–3, 107
mistakes 6, 8–9, 29, 39, 53, 83, 97
models 81
  astronomical 90–3
modernity 4, 11, 57, 121–2, 127
Mohists 17, 27
monarchy 42, 45
monkeys 30, 48
monoculturalism 122
mononaturalism 122
monotheism 97, 101
morality 47–8, 61, 63, 66, 81, 89,
    110–11, 114–15, 120–1, 124
morphology 31
motives 58, 61, 97–8, 113
multiculturalism 122
multinaturalism 122
murder 108
music 17, 63, 82, 116, 119–20, 123
mysteries 37, 39, 104–5
mystical notions 21
mystics 51, 103
mystification 58, 105
myth 16–19, 129

naive understanding 69
naturalism 121–2
naturalists 24, 27–8, 68
nature 21, 25, 28, 54, 68–9, 74, 84, 86,
    88, 93, 96, 105, 124, 129
navigation 68
Neanderthals 30, 113
necessity 85
nomos (law, custom, convention)
    68, 112
norms 9, 43, 110, 115
number 33, 72–4, 76, 78, 80, 82, 90,
    93–4, 105, 127
nurture 68–9

obedience 111
objectivity 32, 34, 68, 122
observation 21, 64, 83–4, 88, 90, 128

Printed and bound by CPI Group (UK) Ltd, Croydon, CR0 4YY